Made in Wombourne

British Library Cataloguing in Publication Data
A catalogue record is available for this book from the British Library

ISBN 978-0-9926031-9-9

Ellingham Press, 43 High Street, Much Wenlock, Shropshire TF13 6AD
www.ellinghampress.co.uk

Cover by Aardvark Illustration & Design
www.aardvarkid.com

Typesetting by ISB Typesetting, Sheffield
www.sheffieldtypesetting.co.uk

Made in Wombourne

Wombourne History Group

Ellingham Press

Dedication

To May Griffiths, MBE, Wombourne's acknowledged village historian, without whose pioneering work over the last seventy years on every aspect of local history we, the villagers, and the village we live in, would all be so much the poorer. The years she spent researching detail and recording her findings have provided an archive of local information and inspired each of us to continue the work she started.

Contents

Acknowledgements

Derek Aldridge, for original photographs of the Seisdon Workhouse.

John Bowler, whose original drawings of many of the buildings first appeared in *Grapevine*.

Burroughs Communications, for permission to use their map of Wombourne.

May Griffiths, MBE, for access to, and use of, her collection.

Paul Hadfield, for original drawings.

Julia King, for proofreading and editing the early drafts of the book.

Hilary Moore, clerk to Wombourne Parish Council, for unstinting help as well as her listening skills.

Benedict Orbell, for help with photography.

Carolyn and John Phillips, for information and permission to use photographs of Wombourne Wodehouse.

SSCVA, for financial support.

Staff at Wombourne Library, for ready support and much photocopying.

Staff at Staffordshire County Archives.

Ina Taylor of Ellingham Press, whose help and enthusiasm for the project has seen me through moments of panic.

Joan Tyson, for assistance with, and providing, illustrations.

Anthony Unwin, chairman of WHiG, and all the other members who have tolerated with great good humour my incessant bullying.

Barbara Webb, the editor of *Grapevine*, for generously allowing us to use illustrations which were first made for that parish magazine.

Members of the Wellings family, for permission to use hitherto unseen material from their family archive.

Wombourne Parish Council, for their very generous financial support.

And many other people, including my long-suffering husband and children, who have given time, help and moral support to this project and to whom I remain deeply grateful.

Margaret King
April 2014

Introduction

WHiG (Wombourne History Group) developed from a working party set up in 2008 to create a Local History Room in Wombourne. This was primarily to house copies of research material gathered by May Griffiths, MBE, over many years, but the collection rapidly expanded to hold all sorts of documents, books and pictures about Wombourne, its neighbouring villages and the surrounding area: a true 'local collection'.

A small room was found to serve as a Local History Room in the Community Centre; this building is owned by Staffordshire County Council and also houses the library, but is separated from it and in a different part of the building. Much of the contents of the History Room, opened in 2009, does not belong to SCC, is not legally the responsibility of library staff and there were not enough volunteers to keep the room open at all times. We began to realise that our collection was not being used enough. If people could not use the 'archives' we would have to make some aspects of it more widely available. Some of us had already written 500-word leaflets about various aspects of the village, under the umbrella of WSS (Wombourne Scientific Society). These had been well received and the idea of producing a book arose from this.

WHiG's objective was to write something about the village which would interest our potential readers as well as us, the writers. It also had to be based on original research and not regurgitated from the internet! Eight of us volunteered, or were 'persuaded', to have a go. We chose subjects in which we were most interested and agreed a time limit for the first drafts to be ready for discussion.

Although writing dissertations and reports, marking homework and producing written work were all in a day's work for many of us, only one of us had been involved in producing a book. It quickly became obvious that the standard model of historical progression from prehistory to modern times was impossible. Styles of writing differed wildly, research methods varied and no unified house style of writing could be achieved without losing the flavour of each contributor's writing. Drafts circulated for criticism, time limits became stretched, but it is to the credit of all WHiG members, including those who were *not* writing text, that we did not lose sight of our objective or the belief that we would, ultimately, produce 'The Book'. Here then you have it, *Made in Wombourne*, faults, warts, blemishes and all – rather like the village itself.

It was a real 'local community' effort, supported by many people, those whose names appear in the Acknowledgements and many others whose names may have been omitted. If they have, it is not out of ingratitude, but lack of space.

Nature's Building Blocks

Philip Pennell

Until the middle of the twentieth century, the *raisons d'être* for the situation and growth of settlements which were mentioned in the Domesday Book were the structure, relief and drainage of the land in the vicinity. This is particularly true of Wombourne as Angus Dunphy pointed out in his 1972 thesis on the parishes of Wombourne and Lower Penn.

The village is situated on sandstone beds laid down in the Triassic period, which overlay the coal measures beneath them. These are the same coal measures which led to the creation of the Black Country to the east of the village. Fortunately there are two fault lines situated to the east of the A449 which means the coal under Wombourne is too deep to mine, otherwise the settlement would have been swallowed up in the conurbation.

The general relief of land in the area results in the drainage pattern being towards the south-west, eventually joining the River Severn at Stourport via the River Stour. The two brooks which were the most important in the continuance of the village are Wom Brook and Smestow Brook, both of which fed the several mills which were situated in the village up to the nineteenth century (although the one in Swindon did not close until the latter half of the twentieth century). This drainage pattern was also responsible for the Staffordshire and Worcestershire Canal passing through the area, as Brindley always followed natural watercourses when routing his canals.

The sandstone beds were first used as the source of building materials, as can be seen at the church. Later the sand was quarried for foundries and used in the building industry. The extraction of sand in the village lasted until the middle of the last century. The sandstone beds were also important for their ability to store water. Thus the Black Country town of Bilston obtained its water supply from Wombourne (thanks to the skills of the Victorian engineers) and the village was provided with a superb building in the ornate style of the late Victorian era.

The Industrial Revolution meant that the village was located next to the iron-making area (which became known as the Black Country), leading to the villagers adding nail-making to their activities.

In the middle of the twentieth century the village's role changed, and this time the physical features in the area were not a feature when the settlement became a commuter village with a sudden upsurge in house-building.

Lords of the Manors of Orton & Wombourne and Other Landowners

Anthony Unwin

Mention a manorial estate and most people will think of a church with an adjacent manor house, cottages clustered around a village green, three large unfenced ploughed fields, woodland and pasture. Scattered around the estate, men and women would be working at seasonal tasks as the lord and his lady rode across the surrounding uncultivated land with hawks on their wrists. But who were this lord and his lady? Unfortunately this simple picture often did not exist; reality was far more complicated and variable, especially here in Wombourne. Immediately the question has to be asked, 'What is meant by Wombourne, the village, the civic parish as it is now or was in the past?' The answer is one or all, depending upon circumstances, and so the following account is a much simplified version of events.

In 1086 when the Domesday Book was written Wombourne manor was held by William Fitz Ansculf, as Tenant in Chief and Baron Dudley, directly from King William in return for personal loyalty, and financial and military support. As Tenant in Chief, Fitz Ansculf could have leased some of his properties to sub-tenants on the same terms as he, Fitz Ansculf, owed to the king. In the case of Wombourne it appears that it was retained as a personal property. Orton, as another manorial estate, was also personally held by Fitz Ansculf. Swindon was not mentioned as existing as a separate estate in the Domesday Book, but was counted as part of Himley manor.

From 1086 onwards the ownership of the original Saxon estates becomes very complicated; estates could be bought and sold by the tenant in chief or sub-tenant and yet ultimately remain the property of the Crown. It was also possible for an estate to become a bride's dowry, which immediately upon her marriage became her husband's possession. Thus it was that when Maud, daughter of Richard d'Offini, lord of many estates (including Orton), married Alan of Orton in about 1220, the Orton estate which was her dowry became his possession.

As a consequence, for the next hundred years or so, Alan's family were known as de Orton. Alan's wealth and influence increased some time later when he acquired the manors of Swindon and Oxley. In 1339, when the Orton estates were sold, most of ancient requirements of personal loyalty, financial and military support had been bought out, so that those in possession of an estate were able to sell all or portions to anyone with the available cash. Here was a chance for successful merchants, tradesmen and farmers to become 'gentry'.

However, it appears that the Orton estate was bought as a whole by Sir William Shareshull of Shareshill. As this estate lay alongside the Trysull estate's eastern border it may explain why, according to Revd Stebbing Shaw, author of *The History and Antiquities of Staffordshire*, the Shareshull heraldic shield was depicted in one of Trysull church's windows. Although the precise date is not known, sometime around 1370 the Everdon family held Orton and continued to do so for the next hundred years, until it came into the possession of the de Grey family of Enville. In 1633 Ambrose Grey got into serious financial trouble and was forced to sell Orton and Seisdon to the Wrottesley family of Wrottesley Park. For the next three hundred years the estates remained more or less intact with the Wrottesleys, until financial problems, mostly death duties, were resolved in 1929 by selling individual buildings and land.

In the 1500s an estate, known as the manor of Wombourne, consisting of scattered properties in Wombourne, Seisdon and Trysull, was held by Sir Roger Hillary of Bescot. His descendants sold it in 1619 to John Woodhouse, who with his financial partner John Huntbach sold it in 1641 to Sir William Wrottesley.

Yet another estate consisting of properties in Orton and Wombourne was held by John Buffery of Lower Penn, which formed the dowry of his daughter on her marriage to Thomas Burnett. This estate was sold in 1608 to Hugh Wrottesley.

The Wodehouse estate had very mundane beginnings. A certain cook called William was granted land in Wombourne by his lord and master William d'Offini at some time between 1176 and 1179. Two assarts were also granted to William the cook. Assarts were land that had been taken out of the common land, fenced and cultivated, then legalised by a fine imposed by the manorial court. According to the *Victoria County History of Staffordshire* the inheritance and identity of possessors of the Wodehouse property and land become very obscure in the late 1300s and 1400s, but by 1688 Edward Woodhouse had died amidst many financial problems. Presumably Edward's son, John, mortgaged the estate to raise the cash to enable life to continue, so that his son and heirs inherited an indebted estate. Samuel Hellier, a London brewer and relative of the original mortgagees, bought out their shares. Hellier then foreclosed, that is, called in the

The parish church of St Benedict Biscop, Wombourne.

original debt which could not be met. He thus possessed the estate and became a 'landed gentleman', later with armorial bearing.

Although buried at St Benedict Biscop's church Samuel Hellier never lived at the Wodehouse, but his son and grandson, both named Samuel, did. This last Samuel never married and on his death in 1784 left the estate to his friend the Revd Thomas Shaw on the quite commonplace condition that he changed his name to Shaw-Hellier. The estate then passed on for three generations to Col. Thomas Bradney Shaw-Hellier, who died without issue so that the title to the estate went to his sister's son Evelyn Simpson. Once again this latest recipient of the estate took the surname Shaw-Hellier. Both of his daughters succeeded to the title to the estate, dying unmarried and without issue. Finally, in 1981, the estate passed to a distant relative, John Phillips, who has retained his own surname.

From the 1700s onwards energetic families began to form estates by cash purchase, the cash originating from their successful businesses, or by mortgaging property already owned. Another device to raise actual cash was to sell annuities to anyone wishing to purchase, the annual payments coming from the rents of the estate newly acquired. During periods of economic stability this system worked well, but if for any reason the rents from the estate dwindled but the annual annuity payments had to be made, then the estate itself would have to be sold. These newer estates were not manorial in character, that is, tenants' rents were paid in cash and not in kind or free labour or service in manorial courts. However, it should be noted that the church tithes continued to be partly paid in kind until the middle of the nineteenth century.

Several examples of the non-manorial estate were created in Orton and Wombourne in the late 1500s and on into the 1800s. The Marsh family held scattered properties and pieces of land, to which succeeding generations added whenever possible, so that by 1816 Richard Bayley Marsh held almost 400 acres. He lived in what was known as the Manor House, now the site of the Wombourne tennis, bowls and cricket clubhouse. The Marsh family also owned Lloyd House and occupied Orton Grange. A similar estate was created by John Smith, father and son, who made their money in the London law courts. Not only did they hold properties in Wombourne and Orton but also in Seisdon where they built Lane End farm, now known as Lanes Farm. The title to this portion of the estate enabled William Tennant of Shenstone, a distant relative, to benefit in 1774 from the enclosure of Seisdon common. The whole of the Smiths' estate was sold to Richard Bayley Marsh in 1818.

In 1899 Harriet Bradney-Marsh, heiress to the combined Marsh and Smith estates, married Col. Shaw-Hellier of the Wodehouse, so that their joint estate covered almost the whole of the northern part of the present civic parish of Wombourne. However, this situation did not last as the Lloyd portion was sold by auction in 1901. A considerable part was purchased by Col. Ward of Bearnett House, who already owned property and land in Wombourne. This last estate was sold and broken up in 1924, thus leaving the Wodehouse portion as the sole intact survivor of the ancient estates.

Information extracted from the Victoria County History of Staffordshire, Vol XX.

A Social History of Wombourne

Margaret King

Those interested in the history of early Wombourne (with or without the final 'e') have to scratch around for evidence. Unlike some parishes, we have few early records. It is also dismaying to discover how seldom Staffordshire, let alone Wombourne, is mentioned in reference books or even in early historical records. There is even less archaeological evidence remaining. Before the 1914–18 war it appears to have been a small, unpretentious and unassuming village, although not without charm. From the 1950s onwards large areas of the parish were developed, fast, either as domestic or industrial estates. The resultant urban sprawl has led to Wombourne, with a population of some 13,000, being called 'the biggest village in England'. These facts conspire to make writing a 'history' or an 'account' of Wombourne imprecise, particularly before the eighteenth century, and thus likely to be overfull of unsatisfactory expressions such as 'maybe' and 'it is likely that ....'.

The pre-Norman history of Wombourne is minimal. Part of a 2,000-year-old sandstone quern (now in the museum in Bridgnorth) was found in a quarry near Smestow in 1944. We have no hard evidence about a Roman Wombourne, although there is a field behind Pickerill's Hill called 'Roman Ell'. (An 'ell' in Shropshire means a slope and Anthony Unwin thinks we should consider that this site might have been used for occupation then.) Wombourne is on the route between the A5 and Greensforge, near Swindon, where archaeological excavation *has* yielded evidence of Roman military forts and roads. In the sixth century Saxon invaders, originally from Denmark, who had fought their way westwards across the centre of England in search of new land, must have found the abundant water and light sandy soils round Wombourne to their liking. With wood, coal and iron in the immediate locality they probably established a small village quite soon after their arrival on the banks of the local streams which we now know as the Smestow, the Smallbrook and the Wombrook.

Living in wooden houses enclosed by thorn hedging, these people undoubtedly kept pigs; Swindon and Kingswinford are local settlement names which support this claim, and the local woodland would have provided good supplies of food for herds of pigs as well as timber for building and fuel. The villagers almost certainly had cattle, sheep and bees as well. They would have grown hemp, flax and vegetables such as peas, beans, turnips and cabbage, whilst barley would have been the main cereal crop. All these were probably grown using the three-field system, but evidence of this is hard to prove. No ridges and furrows remain. Grain was probably ground by hand or in mills powered by the local streams. The village blacksmith would have made iron tools and weapons; quantities of slag are still being found near the banks of the stream (although when that was produced is difficult to prove). Salt was essential for daily life and this had been produced in Cheshire even in prehistoric times. Droitwich, another salt-processing town, called in the Mercian charters *vico emptorio salis*, lies less than 30 miles south of Wombourne, so villagers probably had fairly good access to this vital preservative.

Michael Wood quotes a contemporary text which gives details of food rent for a ten-hide estate in about AD 780.[1] In return for a gift of land from King Aethelbald of the Mercians (Mercia: the land between Oxford and Chester) the landowner was expected to provide honey, loaves, ale, geese, hens, cheeses, butter, salmon, fodder and eels. Wombourne landowners, on less generous land, might have hoped for more modest demands.

In the Dark Ages, following the collapse of the Roman Empire, Staffordshire was part of the Mercian kingdom, but so near to the flexible boundaries between the kingdoms of Mercia, Wessex and the Welsh that it must have been fought over constantly before Wessex became the final victor around AD 900. The Battle of Tettenhall in 910 must have been one of the last fought between the Norse invaders and the combined forces of Mercia and Wessex. Although literacy in Alfred's Wessex was important and fairly well established the kings of Mercia do not seem to have had much time for it. Few written records remain about their kingdom, although the Beowulf legend may have been told in the king's Great Hall in the Mercian capital of Tamworth. Instead we have the Staffordshire Hoard of gold and garnets, consisting almost entirely of decorative items for men's weapons, the discovery of which supports the warlike exploits of the Mercian kings, although the find raises as many questions as it answers.

The Domesday record of 1086 is the earliest written evidence we have of Wombourne when the village is described as having '7 hides of land, 8 ploughs, worth £3.0.0., 13 villagers [only heads of households were counted so probably some 40 souls], a priest and 2 mills'. William I was concerned to guard danger points within his newly acquired territories by giving land to trustworthy individuals, who built castles to protect boundaries, including that with Wales. Dudley Castle is the nearest to Wombourne. Although Stenton claims that 'the new society of the Norman age ignored the ancient divisions of shire and hundred', probably little changed locally.[2] Salt, a vital necessity for food preservation, probably came from Droitwich. There had been salt-processing centres there even through the Dark Ages and this continued under Norman rule, although the Cheshire salt industry was destroyed in an effort to subdue the area.

By 1189 there is a record of the church at Wombourne being built (or rebuilt) by the prior of Dudley and strong ecclesiastical connections with Dudley continue right up until the end of the nineteenth century, at which time the curate of Bilston owned much land in Wombourne. In 1234 the vicar of Womborne is 'given 10 trees from the Forest of Kinver for making beams for his Church which had lately suffered in a fire'.[3]

Medieval people who fell on hard times were probably supported by their neighbours, by the Church (who owned a fifth of all the land in the kingdom) and by the local landowner. He had a vested interest in keeping his workforce reasonably fit for work and (later) for paying rent in lieu of providing labour. 'The core idea behind the feudal system was that those with land and power claimed the right to the labour and surplus of the bulk of the population.'[4] About AD 1130 during Henry I's reign, in Dorset, 'a villein in return for a yardland did 3 days' work a week, paid 7 pence halfpenny, ploughed an acre and a half and harrowed an acre, rendered a measure of corn and 10 pence for wood to repair his house and fences.'[5] The villein in Wombourne, in less fertile Staffordshire, is unlikely to have been expected to achieve that much, but 'he could not leave his home to take up land elsewhere. In law he was bound to the soil of his native manor.'[6] That must have meant desperation for the poor between 1315 and 1320, the years of the 'Great Famine'.

A tithe, a tenth part of people's income, was taken from everyone, either in money or in kind, for taxes and for charitable purposes, including supporting the poor and needy, as well as to meet the needs of pilgrims. Pilgrimage was as important to medieval man as making the hajj is to Muslims today and it is now thought that movement about the country was quite common. When the Plague (a rat/flea-carried bacterium), with all its attendant horror, arrived in the Midlands in 1348 it is likely to have decimated the population of Wombourne as it did everywhere else, but the main effect of the deaths was in terms of the social impact on the workforce. With one-third, or even as much as a half, of the country's total population dead, labourers were, for the first time ever, free to move away and offer their skills elsewhere, for a wage, including to towns such as Coventry.

If the Norman invasion and the Plague, followed by social upheaval, are the first major events that we know affected Wombourne, the next two are basically religious. The Church was such a force in the life of medieval people that today we can hardly comprehend its effect on daily life then. Despite the opportunities available after the 1360s the Church remained the mainspring of people's lives: it ruled their daily existence, caring for the souls and spiritual needs of all and for the bodies (and minds) of the sick, the destitute and the dying. Wills are splendid sources of information about bequests to the poor – and to the Church. However, this same management of estates and money contributed towards the deterioration of the Church, which became fat, greedy and corrupt. The Lollards were the first English dissenters. John Wycliffe, their leader, was a priest in Lutterworth, Leicestershire (from whence one of our village priests, Ithiel Smart, came three centuries later), but his, and their, influence gradually spread throughout the country, resulting in the Peasants' Revolt of 1381. Dissatisfaction with the old order of lords and the Church became a feature of the next century.

By the 1530s no one hearing rumours (and there must have been many even in rural Staffordshire) about King Henry VIII and his marital troubles could have predicted that subsequent events would so alter the way of life in England. 'The sixteenth century in England was a time of great social and economic change. In the countryside arable land was increasingly being converted to pasture, resulting in a reduction in the amount of agricultural labour required.'[7] The break from the Church of Rome finally freed Henry from papal constraints. Henry's subsequent dissolution of the monasteries, which included acquiring their treasures, lands and money, led to a major breakdown of many of the social support systems which had developed over the previous centuries. Without the monastic system people were thrown almost entirely on their own resources for caring for the sick, the orphans, the old and the incurably ill. By the time Henry's daughter Elizabeth came to the throne England had swung violently several times between Roman Catholicism and Protestantism. With Elizabeth's accession Rome finally lost the battle. Out went the universal use of Latin in church and the law; out went wall paintings (Claverley church still has splendid examples), stained glass, icons, statues and the old familiar comforts of the Church. The Poor Rate, a local tax based on the value of the property in which each contributor lived, was passed in 1572. This continued under different names – 'the rates', then the community charge, now the council tax. England became overtly Protestant and by 1593 'the most extreme anti-Catholic Act of all is passed. Those not attending church for a month are to be imprisoned... Just 35 years see Catholicism change from being the respectable norm to the religion of a persecuted minority.'[8]

England under Elizabeth became embroiled in conflicts with Catholic countries, particularly with Spain and her ally Ireland. This placed a huge burden on the exchequer and with economic downturn unemployment became endemic. In 1597 and 1601 Poor Law Acts placed responsibility for poor relief in the hands of each parish. Laws against vagrancy were severe: if people were caught begging they might get a two-year prison sentence and the possible loss of a nose or a hand. 'Hark, hark, the dogs do bark, the beggars are coming to town' dates from this era. Ironically it was at this time that we get the first really useful written records which allow us to say with certainty, 'In Wombourne we did this.' The first parish records which we have are dated 1570 and we get little scraps of social history in asides provided by the parish priest amongst the entries for baptisms, marriages and deaths. It is mainly from these registers that we find evidence about population expansion in England.

There were about 3.16 million people at the beginning of Elizabeth's reign (1533) and 4.11 million at the end (1603), an increase of some 30%. Boys and girls under 16 accounted for 36% of the entire population, but even in rural areas 21% of children died before the age of 10, two-thirds of them in their first year of life and half of these in their first month.[9] In 1563 Wombourne parish had 37 households.[10] Assuming a household comprised a husband, wife and five children this would suggest a total population of somewhere about 300 souls; 100 years later (1676) the Compton Census returned 386 people in the parish.[11]

Childbirth has always been hazardous. Complications during pregnancy and delivery killed many women, which accounts for the numbers of wives some men married. If women survived delivery, secondary infections were still a major cause of death for them and for their infants, although country women stood a better chance of surviving delivery than their town sisters. The infectious diseases of childhood which are still with us (measles, mumps, rubella) all took their toll amongst infants and young children as did smallpox, typhus and cholera. Infections, whether primary or secondary, killed many adults and children. Before the discovery of antibiotics these included dental abscesses, bone disease following compound fractures, and a wide range of infections affecting the soft tissues and internal organs of the body. Causes of death amongst men and boys included many accidents at work; on farms these were always higher in the summer, particularly during harvest time. Causes of death noted in the records include 'fall from a cart', 'kicked by a horse' and 'drowned in the brook'. Fire was always a hazard, not least in a village where metalworking was the norm, including in many backyards.

The 1601 Poor Relief Act (a temporary measure not fully rescinded until 1967!) put responsibility for 'the care of the destitute' into the hands of the parish. Money for this had to be raised from householders and collected by a parish official – 'the overseer' – and was distributed as 'out-relief' – handouts, usually money, food, fuel and clothing. Workhouses were more like workshops where the poor were given work and training. The parish priest and churchwardens managed this care and recipients were expected to conform to the practices of the (Protestant) Church. Elizabeth's successor, James VI of Scotland, became James I of England in 1603. He and his son Charles I had close connections with Roman Catholicism, either by marriage or by inclination, so there was greater tolerance of the old faith during their reigns, making Puritans increasingly fearful of a return to the old faith. James and Charles were upholders of the divine right of kings, Charles in particular seeing Parliament as an intolerable challenge to his authority. He ruled England without a parliament for 11 years until his need for money forced him to recall it. By 1632 Wombourne had a Puritan vicar, Ithiel Smart, described in 1644 by the 'Committee for Plundered Ministers' as 'a godly and orthodox divine'. So we know which version of Christianity was preached from the pulpit here at that time, but that not all parishioners supported his extreme views. Indeed it is reported that in 1650 'a churchwarden & two others pulled down the pulpit and reading desk ... and kept out the preacher'.[12] Perhaps it was a visiting preacher who so incensed the churchwarden, or possibly the churchwarden who acted as overseer of the poor in 1648 had been replaced by another who was less sympathetic towards Ithiel Smart.

The increasing antagonism between the two sides finally led to a series of conflicts between 1642 and 1651 known as the English Civil Wars. Battles on English soil, many of them in Staffordshire and the neighbouring counties, led to further social unrest, upheaval and destruction of the 'old way of doing things'. The Civil Wars divided the country, the counties, towns, villages and even families one from another in a way few previous conflicts had done since the days of Stephen and Matilda. Suddenly, not only fighting men were urgently required by both sides, but also weapons. Foundries in the Black Country, at Birmingham, Halesowen and locally at Sedgley, which specialised in making scythes, had plenty of work. So too had the many metalworkers of Wombourne; used to making farm implements, they

The Wombourne Wodehouse, seen across the ornamental lake during dredging in 2004.

must have converted smartly from beating iron ploughshares into making swords, pikes and other implements of war.

About this time the Wombourn Wodehouse was owned by John Woodhouse who had married Mary Huntbach. They had a number of sons, including Walter and Edward, who all predeceased them. In his will dated 20 April 1633, Walter Woodhouse 'late of the City of London, merchant deceased, late brother of Edward Woodhouse did bequeath unto the use of the poor of the parish [of Wombourne] for the purchase of some land and rents to be used for the maintenance of the poore'.[13] The last surviving son, Edward, died of consumption in 1688, leaving no male issue. Thus, left with no direct male heir to inherit his estate, John Woodhouse disinherited his brother, a known Parliamentarian, who would have become his heir and left the Wodehouse to his wife's relation, Edward Huntbach of Featherstone. There is a presumption that both the Woodhouse and Huntbach families were Royalists, although not known to be Roman Catholic.[14] Following the Royalist defeat, and for the next decade, Roman Catholics continued to be penalised. John Dolman, priest at Wombourne (and son of Thomas Dolman of Seisdon) got the rents from the Black Ladies and White Ladies Priories (near Brewood) sequestered from the (recusant) Giffard family, and in 1657 tithes from lands at Chillington were granted to him.[15]

Following the restoration of the monarchy in 1662 interest in science and technology blossomed. Industry developed rapidly with better extraction of coal (later converted into coke) for firing furnaces. The movement from an agricultural to an industrial society accelerated but brought new social problems. The 1662 Settlement Act had 'spelled out who a parish or township was responsible for – namely those who could claim "settlement" there.' Settlement rights included proof of birth in a parish, renting property worth £10 and a number of other criteria. Without proof, people seeking parish relief for hardship were returned to the parish where they 'belonged', thus becoming 'somebody else's problem'. In acknowledgement of the problems which existed at this time 'the Poor in Wombourn' were left an annuity of 20 shillings by 'Edward Bird late of Swindon husbandman' in 1680.[16]

The early eighteenth century brought further rapid changes countrywide, not least to Staffordshire and its neighbouring counties, rich in coal, iron and wood for smelting. Goods and raw materials had to be moved all over the country, in volume, safely and fast. Roads were bad, wagons (and sometimes their drivers) were unreliable, rivers were not in the right places and not always navigable, but canals answered admirably. Navvies using picks and shovels dug a network of these all over the country, including one which passes through

William Wellings and two of his carts outside his workshop.

Wombourne. Landowners, realising that there was more money to be made from extraction of minerals and coal for firing furnaces, forced through a series of Enclosure Acts, excluding the poor from what had been common land. This spelt disaster for tenants who had scratched a living from the land, caused misery for many and hastened the drift from the countryside to towns. 'Throughout the 18th century the land still dictated most people's lives. Great estates straddled the Midland counties and if the landowners owned great reserves of coal, timber or stone they had no snobbery about using them.'[17]

Manufacturing changed from being a 'cottage-based' industry to factory work on large sites, where many men, women and children worked, sometimes in appalling conditions. Locally, industrialisation included ironworking at Ironbridge and in what is now known as the Black Country; pottery was centred in Stoke-on-Trent and Worcester, and mining everywhere that useful material could be extracted. James Keir had a huge soap-works at Tipton covering 20 acres and by 1778 he was exporting boxes of it all over the country. The use of soap made a major contribution to better hygiene and perhaps everyone, including villagers in Wombourne, smelt better as well! Wombourne had few available natural resources and little industry except for metalworking, particularly nail-making, which was often

Wellings' workshop just before demolition in 2012.

Eighteenth- and nineteenth-century dwellings on Gravel Hill. The lower
house is inscribed with the letters ICM and the date 1768.

Nail-makers' houses, but probably not in Wombourne.

a part-time occupation for agricultural labourers. Nails were hand-made by cottagers, often women and children, using small forges in their backyards. Iron rod was delivered by canal boat to wharves and warehouses near Giggetty Lane and the finished nails taken out of the village by the same route.

In 1715 land in Rookery Road was given by John Smith for a site for two almshouses, built in 1716. In the 1780s these became a poorhouse for the parish and later still they were divided into three dwellings. They were eventually sold, first around 1900 to an unknown buyer, then to the Railways Board and again in 1975. They still exist, although much adapted, in private occupation.

The Poor Relief costs in 1776 for Wombourne were £46 6s 10d and for Trysull (with Seisdon) were £25 3s 5d.[18] Life for the agricultural poor continued to get tougher. By 1794/5 there were wars with France, crop failures (due to very low temperatures) and continuing changes in farming practices from arable to grazing with subsequent lack of work for agricultural labourers. The 1803 Poor Relief costs for Wombourne in 1803 had risen to £303 12s 6d whilst for Trysull (with Seisdon) they were £84 1s 1d.[19] In 1792 dividends of £127 11s 10d 3% Consols, purchased with £100, were left to 'the poor of Wombourn' by Sir Samuel Hellier who had died in 1784.[20] He was a descendant of the Huntbach family, one-time owners of the Wodehouse and married into the Hellier family.

Eighteen-sixteen has been called 'the year without a summer'. The volcanic fallout from Tamboro in the Indonesian archipelago caused widespread starvation and disease as crops failed all over Europe. There are newspaper reports of Welsh hill-farmers' families travelling through England begging for food. From 1820 onwards, after the Napoleonic Wars, even harsher conditions led to social unrest and unease. Ratepayers were paying an ever-increasing amount towards the existing poor relief system, and in 1832 a Royal Commission was appointed 'for inquiring into the administration and practical operation of the poor laws'. This body 'took the view that poverty was essentially caused by the indigence of individuals rather than economic and social conditions.'[21] The authors, who were mainly academics, lawyers, churchmen or well-to-do middle-class men, collected evidence from all over the country, but the questions they asked were confusing and the answers capable of being distorted. There is strong evidence that the results were skewed in favour of the answers the commissioners wanted. The result was the 1834 Poor Law Amendment Act. This formed the basis of what became known as the New Poor Law, aimed at creating a national, uniform and compulsory system of poor relief administration under a new central authority, the Poor Law Commissioners (PLC). There were new administrative areas, known as Poor Law Unions, managed by locally elected boards of guardians who managed these, but how the system was managed was left to the discretion of the boards and there were wide variations. 'Out-relief' was no longer provided; instead, the poor became inmates of the workhouse, with all the humiliation associated with it. There were also 'casual wards' or 'spikes' for those tramping the roads between one workhouse and the next. Tramps had a bed of sorts for the night and in return had to undertake some sort of labour, often stone-breaking, before they could leave.

Some parishes, including our local ones, had already combined to provide a place for their poor: 'Wombourn is a large & ancient village... The 2 Townships (Wombourn & Orton) support their poor conjointly, but the 3 manors repair their roads separately.'[22] In 1836 Seisdon Poor Law Union formally came into being. This body first adopted an existing parish workhouse at Tettenhall, but between 1858 and 1860 a new Seisdon Union workhouse was built near Trysull on what is now called Union Lane. In 1865 Poor Law inspector Andrew Doyle collected graffiti from casual wards including Seisdon 'which appeared to have a rather better reputation'. This includes the line '...at the little clean union at Trysull'.[23] The Trysull workhouse seems always to have offered better treatment to the inhabitants, most of whom were destitute widows. This was unusual because most

Seisdon Union Workhouse at Trysull taken in 1964.

workhouses had a preponderance of men amongst the elderly. Workhouses also took in the physically or mentally sick of any age and orphaned or abandoned children. This latter group could be passed on after the age of about eight or ten as domestic servants or apprentices. By 1842 there is a record in South Staffordshire of workhouse boys sent on 'apprenticeships' of up to 12 years working in coal mines. 'There are scarcely any boys in the Union Workhouses... these are sent on trial to the butties between the ages of eight and nine.'[24] One such boy was George Barker of Wombourn. He was aged ten when he was apprenticed from the workhouse to the mine at Wednesfield 'until he was 21'.[25]

Seisdon workhouse finally closed in 1930. Subsequently it was used as a warehouse and later largely demolished.

What we now call public health became a concern, particularly during the epidemics of cholera which raged in large urban areas in the nineteenth century. In 1853 vaccination against smallpox became compulsory for all infants under four months old. This was largely carried out by union medical officers, but other diseases still took their toll. Wombourne undoubtedly had its share of 'pale and interesting' parishioners who coughed with tuberculosis of the lung or limped with bone lesions caused by the same bacillus. The home was still the place for much nursing care for those who had family or good neighbours and even managed to pay for a doctor to visit. The work-house was the last refuge for those who could not. There were three surgeons at Sedgley, according to *Slater's Directory of Staffordshire* of 1864. No doctor appears in the nineteenth-century censuses for Wombourne, although 'the vestry was employing a parish surgeon by 1827 and from 1828 it subscribed to the Dudley General Institution for the Relief of Ruptures'.[26] Mary Guest, 66, wife of John Guest, nail forger, living at Rushford, appears in the 1871 census described as 'occupation midwife' and Ann Powney, 64, as 'nurse servant'. By 1900 there was a 'Seisdon Union Isolation Hospital' (part of the Union work-house) in Bratch Common Road. In it, on 2 April 1911, there was a caretaker, a matron, a servant and five patients.[27] On the same date Trysull workhouse had 81 residents: 40 males, 41 females and Mr Bindschadler, the master.

Mains water was piped into many houses, replacing wells, after the water-pumping station was built in Bratch Lane in the 1890s. Local sewage works were built about the same time. The Great War of 1914–18 caused severe privation, more particularly in towns and cities, but war was followed in 1919 by Spanish flu, which affected young people more than older. It is claimed that this pandemic killed more people worldwide in a year than died of the plague during a four-year span.[28]

Self-help and social care developed further in the twentieth century. In 1901 the Yew Tree Fund, a local friendly society, was run from the Royal Oak at Halfpenny Green and had 400 members,

The Vine Inn before the First World War.

including people from Wombourne. In 1908 the first Old Age Pension Act was passed; the recipients, male and female, had to be over 65 years old and were means-tested, but received a pension of five shillings a week (seven and sixpence for a married couple). Further legislation followed, notably a Contributory Pension Act in 1925 when people paid in 50 pence per week from age 65. The 1930s, followed by the 1939–45 war, was another time of hardship, but in 1945 the Family Allowances Act '...gave families with two or more children a weekly allowance of 5/- for each child after the first'. In 1946 the NHS was founded, replacing voluntary systems and providing 'free' health care for all. Despite coming under increasing pressure this has continued for 67 years. In 1948 the National Assistance Act was passed. Local provision of relief may have been replaced by national systems, but many local charities continued to provide additional help to people who needed it. These included the Saturday Fund in Wolverhampton and the Wombourne Old Folks' Fund, founded in 1964 and wound up in 2000. To this day, many of us still support local charities such as Compton Hospice and other bodies like the Air Ambulance and the Salvation Army. We may not give a tithe, but we do give it voluntarily.

Notes

1. Michael Wood, *The Story of England* (Viking, 2010), p. 66
2. Doris May Stenton, *English Society in the Early Middle Ages* (Pelican History of England, 1951), p. 69
3. *Victoria County History of Staffordshire,* vol. ii, p. 347
4. Michael Wood, *op. cit.,* p. 240
5. Doris May Stenton, *English Society in the Early Middle Ages* (Pelican, 1964), p. 144
6. *Ibid.,* p. 145
7. Peter Higginbotham, *Workhouses of the Midlands* (Tempus Publishing, 2007), p. 8
8. Ian Mortimer, *The Time Traveller's Guide to Elizabethan England* (Bodley Head, 2012), p. 85
9. E. A. Wrigley & R. S. Schofield, *The Population History of England 1541–1871* (CUP, 1981), p. 249
10. *Ibid.,* p. 564
11. A. Whitman & M. Clapison, *Compton Census of 1676* (OUP, 1986)
12. Wombourn BMD Registers
13. Staffordshire Record Office: Wills, Tithes and other documents
14. Information from John Phillips, owner of the Wodehouse Estate in 2012
15. Staffordshire Record Office: Wills, Tithes and other documents
16. Staffordshire Record Office: Parish charities – Bird Charity Trust Deed, doc. ref. no. D3710/6/1
17. Jenny Uglow, *The Lunar Men* (Faber & Faber, 2012), p. 47
18. Staffordshire County Council Education Dept, 'Poor Relief in Staffordshire 1662–1840'

19. *Ibid.*
20. Stebbing Shaw, *The History and Antiquities of Staffordshire* (1801), ii, p. 216
21. Peter Higginbotham, *The Workhouse Encyclopaedia* (The History Press, 2012), p. 232
22. *White's History, Gazetteer and Directory of Staffordshire*, 1834, p. 202
23. Peter Higginbotham, *op. cit.*, p. 55
24. Royal Commission on Children's Employment in Mines and Manufactories
25. Staffordshire Record Office: Index of Admissions to and Discharges from Poor Law Union Workhouses – Seisdon, vol. ref. D4036/2
26. Staffordshire Record Office: Wombourne ch. Vestry minutes 1835–1941
27. Census return, 1911
28. Wikipedia

Further Sources

BENEFACTIONS: Stewponey Societies: Insurance clubs called Stewponey Societies for the improvement of the labouring classes, Staffs. Pp. 119, 120, 123, 182

H. P. R. Finberg, *The Formation of England 550–1042* (Paladin, 1976)

Slater's Directory of Staffordshire, 1864, p. 132: Wombourn inc. Orton 2,004 inhabitants in 1851

Website: Paupers' Cottage 121 Listed Grade-II building

White's Directory, 1834, p. 202

White's History, Gazetteer & Directory of Staffordshire, 1851

William Salt Historical Collection, Staffordshire, 1915, WSL, S. MS 33, p. 371

Wombourne Tithes: 1842 (transcribed MTK, 2010)

What's in a Name? History is in a Name

Anthony Unwin

Place names are fascinating: they commemorate activities, actions, trades, persons and contemporary heroes, in the past or in the present. In a rural setting all pieces of land and their adjacent paths, tracks and roads had names, sometimes of very great age, very obscure and largely forgotten by the present generation. Wombourne is an exception. As a result of an enlightened policy a number of past place names have been given to present-day situations. However, for the local historian there is a wealth of information to be gained from old maps, in particular the Survey of 1800.

As you walk, drive or even cycle around the centre of Wombourne or the surrounding housing estates, it is difficult to imagine how it looked several centuries ago. Even the last sixty years have brought about enormous changes in the landscape. For centuries Wombourne was a small settlement surrounded by unfenced plough land and pasture amidst a sea of forest, heath and marshland, known in the Domesday record as *vasta* or waste.

Some idea of this cultivated area can be gained by noting the position of the various 'gates', that is, where tracks led into the surrounding waste. Bakers Gate was alongside the present Union Lane at Trysull, Farnells Gate was adjacent to Blackpit Lane and its junction with Flash Lane. However, it is possible that these two latter gates were part of the Orton manorial estate, in existence prior to Domesday until the eighteenth century. Eakley Gate was at the junction of Bratch Common Road and Trysull Road, and Blakeley Gate at the junction of Giggetty and Sytch Lanes with Common Road. The present Boss Gate Close marks the position of its antecedent. Brant Gate lay to the south of Woodhill Lane, on the present parish boundary with Himley.

The manorial system of farming, in use for seven or eight hundred years, utilised two, three, four, even five, unfenced, ploughed fields and the 1800 map suggests that Wombourne had four, namely Potteleith, Houndale, Blakeley and Baggeridge. Pottelith, first noted in

23

Hayload passing the Arbourtree.

1316, Pottelight (1336), Puttelich (1334) and Puttley (1800) ran along the crest of today's Pickerills Hill. Holendene, later named Houndel and finally Ounsdale, is comparable with the combined playing fields of Westfield, Ounsdale and St Bernadette's schools. Blakeley Field was undoubtedly in the vicinity of the present crossroads of Giggetty Lane, Sytch Lane and Common Road. However, it is difficult to establish the boundaries of this field as the conformation of the 1800 field suggests that this was originally an enormous field, possibly including all of the present Broadway, Whites Wood with their subsidiary roads, Blakeley Heath Primary School, and all the ground to the south of Sytch Lane down to the parish boundary with Himley. Alternatively, the long, narrow fields covering the present Giggetty Estate present a more plausible addition, with such names as Big Blakeley, Longlands, Black Acres and Bade Brook. The site and size of Baggeridge Field is also open to speculation. Some fourteenth-century documents offer the alternative name of Woodhill Field so that a number of fields on the 1800 map reached by Woodhill Lane (off the A449, at the back of the Red Lion) could be Baggeridge Field.

The long-standing system of farming ensured that the arable land was ploughed by teams of oxen in long, narrow strips, a furrow or furlong (one-eighth of a mile). Much later, fields were enclosed by hedges and fences, giving rise to long, narrow fields such as Chapman's

Early field names.

Furlong and Chapel Furlong at the corner of Orton Lane and Dene Road. The area at the end of the furrow, where the oxen turned around, the 'headland' in present-day speech, was called the butt. Cats Butt and Far Butt were situated on the area now enclosed by the A449, School Road and Gilbert Lane.

After the demise of the open field system, greatly accelerated by various outbreaks of the Black Death in the fourteenth century, the fields were shared out between the villagers who became tenants or outright owners. The portions were then hedged or fenced and given names which may not refer to the original field name. Hungrey Grey and Bad Furlong, part of Houndel Field, referred to the poor soil. Spiteful Gate, in the vicinity of Cannon Road, gives cause for wonder.

Some field names refer to past activities. There are three Brick Kiln Pieces, one adjacent to Withymere Lane where it turns uphill to the Orton ridge, the other on the parish boundary with Sedgley, up the hill from the Wodehouse. The third lies beside Bakers Gate on Union Lane, previously known as Flash Lane. Lime Kiln Leasowe lies alongside the canal, north of Awbridge, presumably so named after the construction of the canal enabling coal, wood and limestone to be brought to this site which does not appear to have had road access. Fields either side of the junction of Ounsdale, School and Station Roads, now occupied by the New Inn and the Co-op cum post office, were named Big and Little Windmill Piece and offer alternative sites for the windmill celebrated in Windmill Bank.

Orton in the 1700s was still a separate manorial estate with three open fields, one lying on the slope from the Hollybush on Ebstree Road down to the canal and was reached from Orton by Cockpit Lane, which in the 1800s crossed the canal by a bridge, now demolished. Low Field lay between Orton Lane at White Cross and the Kingswinford railway line. The third field appears to have been a part of Wombourne's Putley Field.

Although many field names are very mundane, a few attract attention as arcane or inexplicable. Although a Paycocke or Peacock family existed in the village, why should a group of fields between the Trysull Road at Monks Path and the canal be called Paycockes Horn? There is also the field and recently demolished lane, adjacent to Withymere Lane, known as Roman Ell. And who was the 'beggar' of Beggars Bush?

The Wombourne Parish Registers of Baptisms, Marriages and Deaths

Annette Mann

There are three registers of baptisms, but only one each of marriages and deaths:

Baptisms: 1570–1799, 1800–50, 1851–1905
Marriages: 1570–1902
Deaths: 1570–1939

These registers were copied and transcribed by May Griffiths, MBE. They were typed by Pam Purves, put on to CD-ROM by Ted Robins and checked by David Hill.

In the history room in Wombourne Library there is a file of photocopies of originals 1570–1699 with a marvellous and enlightening preface by May Griffiths. The originals are now in the County Archives at Stafford.

There is also an index of the registers, alphabetically ordered, by Ted Robins, which gives some indication of the most 'popular' surnames in Wombourne.

****

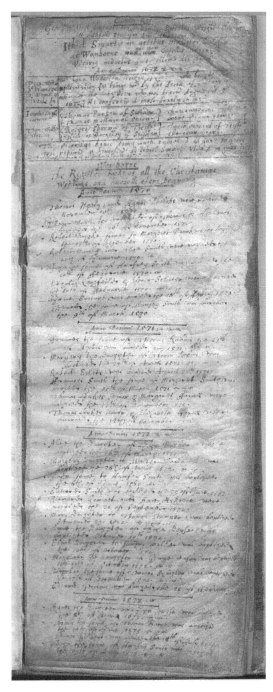

The first surviving page of the BMD Registers in Wombourne. Entries for
1570 copied by Ithiel Smart in 1652.

Baptisms

The early records tell of a child as 'daughter (or son) of...' and no mother's name is given.

Soon there are more details:

1574: *John, son of Joane Walker a waifareing woman*
Elizabeth, daughter of Robert Smith, of Orton
28th Nov. *Elenor, daughter of Humfrey Smith, weaver*
29th Feb. *Richard, son of Humfrey Smith, Milner*
1575: *John, son of Thomas Bull and Elizabeth Huffyall Illegitimately borne*
1575: 7th May *Fraunces, daughter of Richard Becke and Elnor Griffin (baptised and buried)*
9th May *Elnor, daughter of Richard Becke and Elnor Griffin (baptised and buried)*
1586: *John, son of John Bate alia Smith*
Magdelen, daughter of?
1590: *John, son of John Astley at the parish of Womborne*
Elizabeth, daughter of Grace Web a supposed bastard whose father was one William Smith (buried two days later)
1599: *Robert, a base son of Robert Hopkis (supposed father) and Elizabeth Turner*
Jane, a base daughter of James Flynwood (supposed father) and Elizabeth Clarke
1601: *Thomas, son of William Dudley, gent*
In this year, of eleven entries, seven name both father and mother.
1602: *Nicholaus and Izbell, son and daughter of William and Mary Whitemore*
1603: *Fortune, daughter of Anthony Hamnet, vicar*
1605: Anthony Hamnet and his wife had a son, Richard, and in **1606** another son, Gaywood. Two more sons followed in **1623** and **1625** but in **1631:** *John, son of Anthony Hamnet, vicar of Womborne buried Feb. 19th.*
In **1604** comes the first mention of the father's occupation: Elnor and Joane, daughters of John Jeffries, *an hammerman*
1605: John, son of Foulke Browne, *a collier*
In these years there are entries for *filius / filia populi* – children of the parish, presumably born in the workhouse.
In the years **1616** and **1617**:
*Memorandum – that in the old Register Books the years **1616** and **1617** were so confounded together that I could not distinguish them, or else through the carelessness of the vicar or his curates, the burials christenings and marriages were not*

registered, else I for my part have timely recorded what ever I find written – Ithiel Smart (Ithiel Smart was a puritan vicar who had two spells as parish priest in Wombourne). In fact **9** baptisms, **2** marriages and **9** deaths were recorded.

From **1626** the family's place of residence is recorded:

Of Orton, of Swindon, of Envill of ye parish of Enveild, of Womborne, of Wolverhampton, of Hounden, of Hounder, att ye Woodhouse...

From Willenhall, of Sedgley, of the Nether Hamber at Tresle, of ye field, of Clapp Gate, of Himley, of Lower Penn

As well as *a hamberman* we read of a *fyner* and a *milner*.

By **1634** both mother and father are usually named and in **1636** Ithiel Smart and his wife Dorcas had a son Ithiel and in **1637** a daughter Elizabeth, in **1638** Mary, in **1640** Dorcas and in **1641** Katherine.

From **1653** dates of birth are given as well as baptisms, which usually took place within a few days, though in **1654** on 2 November fourteen children were baptised, whose births are registered from October to March. This practice seems to have ended in **1659**, started up again in **1694**, then lapsed in **1726**, viz:

1678: *Anne, daughter of John and ... Shackspear her mother buried at the same time.* (How sad that this woman died giving birth, yet was not even named in the register.)

1714: Francis and Abigail Sadler charmingly named their twins Mary and Joseph.

There was at least one 'base child' a year, or a 'base son' or *'ye base daughter'*.

Other details:

1785: *David, son of William and Eleanor Thomas settled to this place*

1806: *Esther, daughter of John and Esther Pilsbury, born and privately baptised April 6th.*
Fully baptised July 20th

1810: *James, son of James and Isabella Timewell, of the Queens Own Light Dragoons*

1812: on December 30th Thomas and Sarah Vernon had three children baptised:

Thomas, born 19th January 1809

Mary Ann, born 25th December 1810

Harriet, born 18th September 1812

One wonders what the reason was for these three children being baptised together.

On the last page of the **1812** baptismal register we read:

Ann Harris, the wife of John Harris of Monmore Green in ye township of Wolverhampton, collier, maketh oath that on ye

18th day of January last, she was delivered of a male child,
baptised by ye name of John, ye four days after ye said child
was born, she delivered him to Frances, the wife of Foxall
Cartwight of Wombourn in the same county, Farmer, [commas
as I have printed here, as in my original copy. A full stop after
'county' does not make sense] *who promised to support and*
provide for it.
Sworn before one of His Majesties Justices of the Peace for the
County of Stafford.

Another story to be unravelled?

From **1813**, as well as the father's and mother's names, there is a
column for the place of birth and another for occupation. So now
we have *Boatman, Carpenter, Tailor, Labourer, Millwright, Nailer,*
Forgeman, Cooper, Servant, Wheelwright on the first page alone!

As the years go on there are many labourers but also *Tool grinder,*
Blacksmith, Joiner, Victualler, Besom maker, Farmer, Nail factor.

There is also now no mention of illegitimacy: simply the mother's
name and, under occupation, *spinster.*

1814: *a woman in the almshouse who breeds children in the absence*
of her husband
More occupations are noted: *Locksmith, Butcher, LockKeeper,*
Gardener, Crock Seller, Sawyer, Forge Carpenter, Thresher in
the Machine (**1816**).
William Beavon of Heath Forge was a *Stock Taker.*
We have a *Blade Grinder, Cordwainer* (one at Swindon, one at
Houndel), *Excise Officer, Shoe Maker, Glazier, Scythe Grinder,*
Tool Grinder, Earthenware Man.

1820s: the registers still record mostly Wombourne residents but as
well there are people from Lloyd Lane, Dudley, Kidderminster,
Black Lake (Blackley/Blakeley?), Smester, Gigatree, Dibdale
nr. Sedgley. Edward Crockitt, ironmaster, lived at *Graveyard,*
Sedgley. Thomas Baylis of *Botram* was a *Huckster,* but an
Anslow and a Cartwright were both *Gentlemen.*
Samuel Price Edwards of St Benets, Paul's Wharf was a *han-*
dling master to H.M. Customs. Why did he and his wife Jane
come to Wombourne to have their son Samuel Martin baptised
in **1826**?

1827: Samuel Price Edwards is now from Shoreham in Sussex and
is a *Collector of H.M. Customs.* He and Jane come up to Wombourne again for the baptism of their daughter Jane Parker.

1829: Samuel is still a Collector of Customs at Shoreham and he and
Jane come to Wombourne again with their latest son Bevan
Lister.

1834: Samuel is still at Shoreham, still a Collector of Customs and his son Corbett, born August 1st, **1830**, is baptised at Wombourne on August 24th and on November 17th James Bevan is baptised.

1830: 2nd March, Clarinda Adeling is born to John William Rowarth and his wife Ann Shaw of the Woodhouse. He was a captain in the 11th Regiment MN East India Service. What a contrast to the child of Ann Williams and William Huselbee, who was born to a labourer and a carpenter of Ladywell Cottage!

More occupations: a *Gamekeeper* from Swindon, a *Groom* from Greenhill, a *Coachman* from Dudley, a *Miner* from Tipton...a *Moulder*, a *Puddler*, a *Coal Heaver...*

1834: there are alas recorded two *illegitimate daughters* and one *base son, the reputed father in jail for bigamy.*

1836: Thomas Bradley Shaw, son of Thomas Shaw Hellier and Alice of the Woodhouse has *a gentleman* for a father, as has the child of Ralph Gough of Heath House (**1834**).

1837: amongst the Janes, Elizabeths, Susans and Marys the daughter of *a clergyman* is baptised Emily Matilda, and the schoolmaster Thomas Booth and his wife Harriett name their daughter Sarah Hannah.

1842: during August and September were the baptisms of the children of two *Nailers*, one *Labourer*, one *Bricklayer*, one *Clerk to the Canal Company* and the *Vicar* of Wombourne.

1845: another contrast – the children of John Dudley of Greenhill and John Stephens of Beggars Bush, *Labourer.*

1846: as well as the usual working-class occupations are William Thom *clerk – curate of Wombourne*, William Beaman – also a clerk and Robert Holmes – a policeman, but Edward Tucker of Ladywell was a shepherd.

1851: Samuel Coates, born in *Montrose, Scotland*, is *an Army Pensioner* – was he engaged in the First Afghan War (1839–42)?

1852: as well as gardeners, labourers and nailers Mary Ann Stanbridge's father was a schoolmaster and Olivia Ann Richards of Woodford Cottages was a commercial traveller, whilst William Jordon of Orton was a *husbandman.*

1859: Mary Evans was *not living with her husband.* In other parts of the register we read of *a married woman living apart from her husband.*

1861: Thomas Chelmick, an *Officer in the Inland Revenue* had his third daughter.

By the 1860s what we would consider to be more modern names are creeping in: Sarah Winnie, Ernest, Minnie Catherine, Alfred.

1862: *Melene Morris*, daughter of John and Eliza Williams of Sedgley, *dispenser of medecine.*

1864: John Bailey was born to William and Naomi of Wombourne, *a Veterinary Surgeon* and in **1865** their daughter Florence (named after Florence Nightingale, heroine of the Crimean War, 1854–56) was born.

1865: John Williams of Blakeley was a *Surgeon's Assistant.*

1866: Martin Maimion was a *Cabinet Maker.*

1867: Harry Engall, son of William and Sophia Ann Harriet Gibbs of Park Villa (metal broker).

October 27th (?) Frederick Thomas Thornbury (born 6th October **1854**) and his sister Charlotte Frances Susanne (born 8th March **1866**) were baptised. They were the children of George Thornbury (*Railway Manager*) and his wife Martha (both deceased). One supposes that their new guardians had these orphaned children baptised.

Wombourne places of residence are specified more often: *Lower End, Wombourne Common, Giggetty, Blakeley, Bratch, Bearnett.*

1869: Mary Jane and William Kimberley, twins of William and Mary Ann Kimberley of Wolverhampton, *porter*

1870: Joseph Mills of Kingswinford, a *Coal Merchant*, and his wife Harriet had their six children baptised on 6th April. They were born in **1862, '64, '67, '68** and **'70**. Another child was baptised in **1873** and another in **1875**. Joseph must have prospered to provide for such a large family!

The same year, when James Cope was baptised, his father was simply *an adult in extreme illness, late a marine, R.N.*

1871: diverse occupations include *charcoal burner, key stamper, park keeper* (at Himley Park).

1874: Enoch and Adeline Moseley of Coseley (*Railway Porter*) had twin sons, Enoch and John.

Girls' names are more elaborate: *Ada Amy Eliza, Alice Annie, Florence Ellen, Gwynieth Emmeline.*

1876: Levi Gadd of Wombourne was a humble nailer but his wife rejoiced in the names of Lucretia Elizabeth and they named their new daughter Minnie Elizabeth.

1877: Thomas Smitherman of Wombourne was *a shearer* but little Louisa Elizabeth Boycott's father was from the Wodehouse, Wombourne and her mother was from *Rudge Hall, Shropshire.*

1878: Fathers' occupations include *Horse Nail Makers, Edge Tool Makers, Iron Fitter, Furnace Man* and *Sheet Roller.*

1879: Edith Adelaide Tongue was named after her mother, but her father William was only a *Stud Groom.* Were they aping their betters? Might they fall foul of...?

1880: Samuel Price – ex-police inspector?

1882: George and Florence were the twins of Lydia and Joseph Holland, *Pork Butcher*.

More occupations: *Newsagent, Woolen Draper, Musician*. In amongst the working-class occupations were the *gentlemen* and those who worked for them.

1888: William Farm, *Toll Clerk* of Ounsdale

1889: Henry Hadley of Netley House, *Manufacturer* (of what?)

1891: Joseph Edward Claridge, *Postmaster* of Wombourne

1897: Edward Dalton *Watchman*

1898: Florence is still a popular name and baby Horace Gladstone Blewitt's father was a (patriotic) labourer from Giggetty.

1900: William Farr was a *Toll Clerk at Bratch Lock*.

This Baptism Register ends in 1905 and on the last page the occupations listed are:

Labourer, Grocer, Waggoner, Labourer, Labourer, Single Woman, Gardener, Boatman, Labourer, Labourer, Labourer, Ships Stoker, Maltster, Labourer, Carpenter, Innkeeper, Boatman, Labourer, Labourer, Labourer, Engineer – a microcosm of life in Wombourne.

The Toll House and canal complex at Bratch Lock.

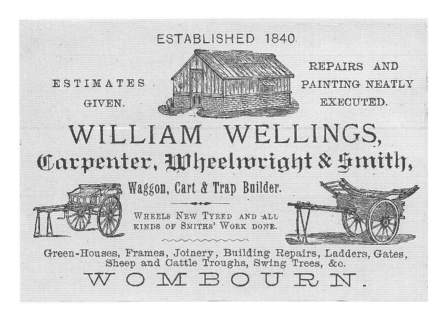

Marriages 1570–1902

Initially the Register shows what we would consider to be only a few marriages a year:

1570: 4
1571: 3
1572: 2

and so on.

In **1602** there were seven! The only details given are the man's Christian name and surname (ditto the woman) and the date of their marriage.

Now and again we read:

married at Dudley
married at Sedgley

And from **1634** there are sometimes more details:

William Baker (Kingswinford)
John Parsons (Tipton)

1638: *John Bache of Wombourne to Anne Wilkes of Dudley*
1651: Thomas Smith of Stourbridge (Oldswinford parish) Elizabeth Woodhouse (of the Woodhouse)

1661: Two marriages at Himley by Licence. One was Robert Smith of Swindon to Elizabeth Buckley of Wombourne (*Widdow*).

There are the usual interesting spellings:

> *Tonfare* (Kinver)
> *Tressel* (Trysull)
> *Taitenhall* (Tettenhall)
> *Worvill* (Worfield)
> *Enfield* (Enville)
> *Bonnigall* (Boningale)
> *Padsall* (Patshull)
> *Swinford Regis* (Kingswinford)
> *Blockwich* (Bloxwich)
> *Shiftnall* (Shifnal)

From **1754** the records are more detailed:

1755: *Francis Dovey of the Parish of Kidderminster and Mary Muchall of Wombourne by Banns, Witnesses Isaac Cartwright and William Sadler.*
Daniel Cartwright of the Parish of Womboume and Ann Guest of Womborn.
The aforesaid were married in the parish church of Womborn p.lie.
This marriage was solemnised between us in ye presence of The mark X of Richard Guest Daniel Cartwright William Sadler Ann Cartwright late Guest

(The rest of the marriage entries have been abbreviated from the above form by me – M.R.G. – for convenience while copying these records.)

Richard Bunce and Sarah Rogus both marked their names with an X. From **1758** there are no Xs and almost all the participants are from *Womborn*, which from **1801** is spelt *Wombourne*.

From **1813** the unmarried state is recorded as *Bachelor, Spinster* and sometimes *Widower, Widow*. (Widowers and widows seem to have married each other quite frequently.)

The words *Banns* (usual) and *Licence* (more unusual) also appear. In **1825** Miss Sarah Shaw Hellier was married by licence.

A new register is begun in August **1837** in which the man's occupation (and sometimes that of the woman) is listed, and also *full age* (which presumably means over 21). Young men and women of 20 or 19 are documented.

From **1848** the register merely states *under age*.

The occupations are the usual *Nailer, Miller, Mechanic* and *Boatman*, with a good leavening of *Draper, Japanner, Glass Cutter, Shoemaker,*

Butcher and associated trades. Women's occupations are *Servant, Milliner, Shopkeeper, Bonnet Maker, Lady's Maid, School Mistress* and *Dressmaker*.

There is a note that, from **September 1866** to **July 1867,** *marriages took place at St John's, Swindon as Wombourne Church closed for repairs.*

From **1864**, though *Full Age* is still common, other ages creep in (most are under 30).

> Edward Milton aged 45
> Elizabeth Wright aged 34 (both widowed)

1871: Richard Haukins 49 *(Widower)*
Maria Marson 33 (*Spinster*)
Some might think that Sarah Ann Taylor (aged 28, father a shepherd) was lucky to catch the 19-year-old William Hollings who was a coachman and the son of a gamekeeper!

1886: Arthur Francis Brown, *Corporal Fourth Dragoon Guard*, whose deceased father was a blacksmith, married Lucy Devey, whose father (also deceased) was a labourer. They were 27 and 28. How long had they been 'walking out' one wonders?

1889: John Lemming (groom) married Sarah Ann Carter (domestic servant). No need to ask how they met!

1890: Did Kate Holloway, aged 23, jump at the chance of marrying Charles Owen (*Saddler*), a widower of 43?

There are human stories such as these, and more, to be found in the pages of the Wombourne Parish Marriage Register.

Burials 1570–1939

Burial records began in **1570**. Very often there are no details, but there are many exceptions:

1587: *Margaret Troughton, a stranger*
Elinor Mathews, widowe
1588: *a poore man unknowne was buryed*
1590: *Elizabeth, daughter of Grace Web whose supposed father was one William Smith (Baptised two days before)*

By **1600** we are given more details: *a miller, Husbandman, a poor labourer, a poore widowe, a poore servant, a poore beggarwoman.*

1633: *a poore blind beggarman that dyed at Swyndon*
1634: *Margaret Buckley, wife of Thomas of Womborne, who broke her legg the Wednesday before, died and was buried the Friday after Mary Hanson who had been a lunatick a long time*

1638: *Thomas Rider, who was strucke blind by God's providence being impatient under his crosse cut his own throat*

1661: *Elizabeth Marsh was carried home and buried at Sedgley. Memorandum yt ye sd.Elizabeth upon discontent ag. ye minister took an oath...never to come to Womborn church more, very shortly after she was struck with a sickness whereof she dyed, and neither came nor was brought to ye church or churchyard*

1674: *Joan Littelford – The old woman of Moises Hall*

1679: *Mr Edwin Smith – my worthy friend*

More details:

1687: *dying by ye fall of an chimney at Swindon*

1689: *kild by his wagon, buried at Himley*

1706: *March 29th – Sarah Shaw*
April 5th – Sarah, base child of Sarah Shaw

1775: *Mary Tongue – wife of William Tongue senior and many years housekeeper to William Lord Dudley and Ward*

1796: *Samuel Rogers crushed under a waggon*

1789: *a poor boy, unknown, burned to death*

There were many burnings and drownings too.

There are a few incomplete entries while the vicar was away serving as a Commonwealth chaplain during the Civil War (1642–48).

Most burials were of local people: *Jigatree, Gigatree, Blakeley Heath, Blackley,* Bull Meadow, Bratch, *Botram,* Greens Forge, Swindon, Seisdon. But some lived further afield: Darlaston, Ettingshall, Sedgley, *Sherif Hales, Boss Gap* (?), Kidderminster, *Enfield* (Enville?), *Rock Houses.*

By **1600** there were more details as to occupation: *miller, husbandman, a poor labourer, a poore servant, a poor beggarwoman.*

Some people lived to a good old age:

1641: John Smith, *being 96 years of age or thereabouts*

1649: Elizabeth Turner, *widdowe aged 90 or thereabouts*

1681: Richard Granger aged 82

1692: Ferdinando Pratt *of Orton, who was reputed to be 95 years old*

1758: Richard Wilson aged 82

1770: Charles Allday, *from Common Side, aged 104*

But many of those who died were children or infants – and some were described as *a bastard, a bastard childe, base childe, baseborne child* – and many women died in childbirth.

All Saints, Trysull.

One exceptionally detailed entry reads:

1649: *Sara Smart, who died at John Grangers of Trysull, where it was put forth to nurse, being three-quarters of a fortnight old, was buried in Trysull chancel*

A note in the registers states:

> *From **1840–60** there were 758 deaths of whom 354 were children under four, so as good as half the deaths in these twenty years were children.*
> ***1859** was the worst year – 54 out of 69 deaths were children, all but one under ten and the majority under seven. 21 were one year and under.*

By **1900** things had improved: of 28 burials 14 were of children under ten. And by 1939 of 24 burials only three were children. After that, with the advent of penicillin and the NHS, the litany of child mortality dropped even further. Each of these child deaths is a tragic family story, but also imagine the emotions of the undertaker who had to make the tiny coffins, the gravedigger who had to dig the tiny graves and the vicar who had to read the prayers over these little innocents!

Analysis of Tithes & Censuses

Margaret King and David Taylor

The giving of a tithe is an ancient custom found worldwide. It seems to be associated with most forms of religion, 'usually as an agreed proportion of the yearly profits from farming'.[1] There are references to tithing in Jewish, Muslim, Greek, Roman and Christian literature as well as in the various religions of India and the Far East.

Tithes, literally a tenth part of everything that was produced from the land – 'all things arising from the ground'[2] – were given to the Church, usually in kind, to support its work, particularly in relation to the care of the poor and needy. Stenton says that 'from the tenth century the payment of tithe by the laity was enforced by the law of the land, but it was only slowly that tithe became part of the endowment of the parish priest'.[3] Even as early as the reign of the Saxon King Edmund *c.* 941, failure to pay had become a matter for excommunication.[4] Tithes were divided into *great* and *small tithes*; corn, hay and wood were considered *great tithes* and everything else *small tithes*.

In good years the tithe might have been given with reasonable grace, much as we now accept paying income tax, although farmers, then as now, grumbled about their loss of income. The problems arose after a bad year. Whether this had been caused by bad weather, sickness amongst farm animals or their human owners, or by any other calamity such as a fire, the obligation to give was still there. Having to hand over the family pig might well bring starvation to a householder. Humanitarian landlords would sometimes waive the payment in such cases, but not all were so well disposed and many smallholders were taken to court for failure to deliver. The Consistory Court records are full of claims relating to property, as land, including what was produced from it, was the major source of income for landowners until the Industrial Revolution.

In 1535 the Great tithes of Wombourne and Trysull were worth on average £10 a year,[5] but there are documents giving much more detailed lists of the money due for every sort of produce. A good example of this is contained in a terrier of the glebe land of the Vicarage of Wombourn written in August 1698:

> ... but for Tyth Hay in Wombourn I have usually Recd. Twelve pence per The Tythes of Wool & Lamb Pigs & Geese Hemp & Flax & Hay are due in kind in Orton and Wombourn But Swindon hath a Custom to pay for hay after two shillings per day Math. If there be seven Lambs One is due the Vic he allowing three half pence which is a half penny a Lamb to make up the number ten. The seventh Pig or Goose is due without any allowance. The custom of Cows and Calves of what Number soever is a penny a Cow & half penny a Calf.

After the Reformation, when much of the property owned by the Church was redistributed either to the Crown or to new (lay) landowners, these new landholders also acquired the tithes which came from the land. In 1541 Wombourne's rectory passed from Dudley Priory to Sir John Dudley and then to the Wrottesley family of Wrottesley in Tettenhall. During the next three centuries, and as agriculture was replaced by industry, tithes were paid in cash (rent-charges) rather than in kind. The system became immensely complicated and pleased nobody. The Enclosure Acts had contributed towards the confusion as one of the objectives of enclosing common land was to get rid of the obligation to pay tithes.

By the nineteenth century, the management of tithes had become chaotic: estates, land (and with that land the tithes due from it) had been merged, divided, sold and resold again, and landowners were deeply dissatisfied with the income tithes brought them. By 1840 Wombourne tithes were being paid to Lord Wrottesley, to John Hill and Thomas Lane (both of Wombourne) and to William Phillips of Enville, as well as to the Vicar of Wombourne. All were receiving rents, charges in lieu of tithes, but 'the sum was found to be below the average paid'.[6]

In order to try and resolve this nationwide problem a bill was brought before the House of Commons in 1836 which sought to commute tithes (i.e. to substitute money payments for payments in kind) throughout the country;[7] this bill became the Tithe Act of 1836. Three Commissioners were appointed to tour the country reviewing each parish and township and finally arrived in Wombourne in 1842. Their investigation produced the greatest in-depth review of the parish since Domesday.

Three copies of their report were made for every parish or township they reviewed: one for the Commissioners in London, one for the diocese and the third to be retained in the parish. Wombourne's parish copy was kept in the safe at St Benedict Biscop Church until placed in the County Archives at Stafford. (A complete transcription has been made by me and a copy placed in the Local History Room in Wombourne.) The original document bound with tape has a very utilitarian brown paper cover over 40 pages. The majority are plain sheets of vellum measuring 540 x 620 mm (18 x 23 inches), but a few, presumably those common to all parishes, have a London printer's address at the top. The document weighs some two kilos and is ruled up and handwritten in ink throughout, except for some of the printer's attributions.

There are four sections:

1. Articles of Agreement: this is a legal document acting as the preamble to the detail of the Tithes Document.
2. The Schedule: this is the equivalent of a modern spreadsheet and divided into columns. The first two are headed *Owners, Occupiers*. There follow eight columns headed *Number referring to plan, Name & descriptions of Lands & Premises, State of Cultivation, Quantities in Statute Measures* (sub-divided into *Acres, Rods and Poles*), *Payable to Vicar, Payable to Impropriator, Names of Impropriator* and finally *Remarks*.
3. The Summary
4. Two Maps: One is of the whole parish and the second is a 'blown-up' map of the centre of the village. Wombourne is extremely fortunate in having very good and well-drawn maps, unlike some parishes which have barely more than a sketch map. There is a unique number for each plot, house, workshop, garden, field and road which relates to the Schedule, allowing the Commissioners, and us, to identify every piece of property.

The 1842 Tithe Commutation enables us, in 2013, to recreate the village of 170 years ago. It gives us the name of the head of each household and shows where they lived (although unfortunately not what their property was called then). We can see what each person owned or rented, where they lived, walked, worked and died. The document we now call the 1842 Tithe document was drawn up for bureaucratic and financial reasons. With it, and with the censuses which followed and which are now available on-line, the Victorians created a goldmine for local historians.

The first recorded Census we have for Womborn (*sic*) is that of 1841. In District 1, which covers only the centre of the village, 841 inhabitants are named and their occupations given. District 2, covering the area outside the immediate centre, is given in a separate table. This census, sketchy though it is, provides us with the first real analysis of what people did for a living, although it might be reasonable to assume that not everyone worked in Wombourne and that the one solicitor listed practised elsewhere. By far the largest group consists of 101 nailers, whilst only 43 call themselves agricultural labourers and 12 'labourers'. There are 23 female servants, but only 6 manservants, (of whom one is nine years old) and 6 gardeners. There are 5 each of blacksmiths, carpenters, clergymen, coopers and shoemakers. All other occupations are in single figures below five but this list of 64 occupations covers everything from army pensioners to woodcutters and includes cripples (1), deaf and dumb (1), paupers (3), widows (4) exciseman (1) and 11 independent.

The censuses which followed every ten years thereafter become increasing full of information about our ancestors, but the detail contained in the 1842 Tithe Commutation document allied to the 1841 Census gives us our first really detailed view of Wombourne.

The delay in compiling the Wombourne Tithe Commutation document in 1842, six years after the Act became law, was due to the time it took the small team of Commissioners to travel around the country undertaking the work. The document analysed here covers only Wombourne parish, excluding Orton, Swindon, Smestow, Hinksford and other neighbouring areas.

It showed that there were 746 plots of land in Wombourne, with a Greater Tithe of £206 8s 9d and a Lesser Tithe of £96 9s 5d. Table 1 suggests that this is about in line with other townships that have been analysed, in particular Ponteland in Northumberland which has features similar to Wombourne in size and occupational base.

Table 1: Comparison of the parish of Wombourne's tithe values

Parish or Township	Greater Tithe	Lesser Tithe	Comment
Wombourne: Staffordshire	£206 8s 9d	£96 9s 5d	
Ponteland: Northumberland	£214 14s 4d	£93 5s 0d	Populous Township
Kirkley: Northumberland	£238 10s 0d	£32 15s 6d	Farming Community
Average of the parish of Ponteland's 8 townships	£260 11s 9d	£37 6s 1d	8 miles north-west of Newcastle upon Tyne
Embleton: Northumberland	£310 3s 6d	£132 0s 0d	Farming Community
Craster: Northumberland	£86 18s 6d	£4 9s 10d	Small Fishing Community
Average of the parish of Embleton's 8 townships	£241 11s 1d	£69 18s 9d	41 miles north of Newcastle upon Tyne
The Northumberland Township information from A. W. Purdue, 'An Oxford College, Two Parishes and a Tithe Farmer: The Modernisation of Tithe Collection', *Rural History*, vol. 8 (1997), pp. 1–19 (p. 12)			

The Right Honourable Lord Wrottesley held £205 17s 3d of the Greater Tithe, John Hill, Thomas Lane and William Phillips held the remaining 11s 6d. There are 746 plots of land recorded, of which 116 had no tithe registered, 364 had only a Lesser Tithe and 266 had both tithes registered. Houses and gardens generally had a

Lesser Tithe of 2d and no Greater Tithe. However, some of the larger houses and gardens, such as Job Baker's property along Botterham Lane which occupied 0.7 acres, incurred a Lesser Tithe charge of 1 shilling and sixpence. Only the larger houses and gardens, usually above 0.5 acres, attracted a Greater Tithe. Presumably this indicates that the house and garden had been built on part of a field that had attracted the tithe in the past. The majority of the properties with no tithe registered to them were houses and miscellaneous buildings, although there were also some of the lanes and parts of the canal land. Of the four nail warehouses identified, only one has a tithe registered against it, that occupied by John Elwell, perhaps because it is described as having a stable attached to the warehouse.

The Greater Tithe was registered against 921 (65.8%) of the 1,400 acres in the parish; of this 887 (96.3%) acres are denoted as arable. There are 998 arable acres in the parish; therefore 88.9% of them are registered for the Greater Tithe. Of £206 8s 9d payable as Greater Tithe, £200 6s 4d (97.1%) is assessed against arable land, at a rate of 4s 6d per acre (see Table 2).

Table 2: Assessment for Greater Tithe by land use in the parish of Wombourne

Land Use	Land Area (a.r.p.)	Greater Tithe (£.s.d.)	Rate Per Acre (£.s.d.)
Arable	887.0.7	200 6s 4d	0 4s.6d
Houses, buildings, etc.	31.2.9	5 9s 8d	0.3s 6d
Nursery	2.1.10	0 10s 10d	0 4s.8d
Garden	0.2.32	0 1s 11d	0 2s 9d
Total	921.2.18	206 8s 9d	0 4s 6d
(a.r.p.) are the statute measurements of area, being acres, roods and perches. There are 4 roods per acre and 40 perches per rood.			

The assessment for Greater Tithes was based on the average price of corn in the previous seven years and the amount of corn produced on the land; it is possible therefore to assess the relative productivity of arable land use in the township. For example, land rated at 3s 0d or less is primarily allotments, occasionally with a small building attached, and they account for 161 acres, an average plot size of 4.2 acres. Land rated at above 6s 0d consists of fields, again with an average plot size of 4.2 acres. Further research may discern further reasons for the differences in productivity.

The Tithe Commutation map can tell us more than who received or paid the Greater and Lesser Tithes. We know that there were 1,400 acres in the parish, of which 73.3% (1,026 acres) was owned by only six people (see Table 3). The Reverend William Dalton was a well-known figure in Wolverhampton and became vicar at Saint

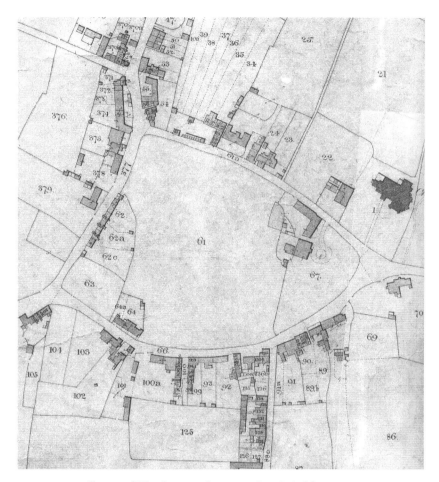

Centre of Wombourne shown on the 1842 tithe map.

Philip's in Penn Fields when it opened in 1859. Thomas Shaw Hellier owned the Wodehouse estate. John Hill lived in Walk House and farmed a substantial acreage in the village. The curate of Bilston also owned land in Wombourne and the reason for this will be the subject of future research.

The majority of the owners would be classified as absentee, not living in the village, and in total 1,279 (91.4%) acres of the township are owned by people who are not resident.

Ten farmers occupy 876 (62.6%) acres, with John Hill, the third-largest landowner, working the greatest area, 189 acres (see Table 4).

John and William Hill lived next door to each other in Middle Street in the 1841 census. It is likely that they were brothers.

Arable farming dominated land usage in the village at 998 (71.2%) acres, which is in line with the dominance of market gardening that

Table 3: List of the major landowners in Wombourne

Owner	Acres	Percentage	Residence
Reverend William Dalton	511	36.5	Not resident in village
Thomas Shaw Hellier	236	16.9	Not resident in village
John Hill	86	6.1	Resident
The curate of Bilston	67	4.8	Not resident in village
The Right Honourable Lord Ward	64	4.6	Not resident in village
The Right Honourable Lord Wrottesley	62	4.4	Not resident in village
Others	374	26.7	
Total	1,400	100.0	

Table 4: List of those farming the greatest acreage in Wombourne

Farmer	Acres	Percentage
John Hill	191	13.7
Peter York	141	10.1
William Hayward	131	9.4
William Hill	126	9.0
Samuel Jones	100	7.2
William Chinner	49	3.5
Joseph Corns Snr	41	2.9
John Cartwright	37	2.6
John Aston Jnr	30	2.1
John Dicken	30	2.1
Others	524	37.4
Total	1,400	100.0

emerged later in the nineteenth century (see Table 5). The 102 (7.3%) acres occupied by housing, gardens, yards and other buildings reflect two overlapping aspects of the village: firstly, the agricultural basis of Wombourne's economy and secondly, that nailing was a domestic industry which required a workshop area. Most of the cottages occupied by agricultural labourers had gardens attached to them, some of which were quite large. John Howell's occupied 0.4 of an acre. Similarly some nailers occupied a large house and garden: for example, Richard Guest's house and garden covered almost 0.4 of an acre. This is substantially larger than that of the nailer Thomas Dean, whose house and garden covered only 0.1 of an acre. It was common practice for people in a rural area, no matter what their occupation, to grow some of their own food in their garden. These factors combined to support the notion that more people lived in Wombourne than a wholly rural parish could support.

South end of old barn and adjacent cottages on the corner of Rookery
Road and Gravel Hill.

Table 5: Land use in Wombourne

Land Use	Acres	Percentage
Arable farming	998	71.2
Housing, gardens, yards, etc.	102	7.3
Pasture	93	6.6
Meadow	92	6.6
Wood and plantation	61	4.4
Roads and associated uses	18	1.3
Pleasure gardens and grounds	16	1.1
Canals and associated uses	12	0.9
Nursery	8	0.6
Total	1,400	100.0

Three properties in the parish are described as 'house, buildings,
pleasure ground'; these include the Vicarage, with three acres, the
Woodhouse, with six acres (including 'Plantations') and Greenhill
Mansion with seven acres (including a paddock). Two nurseries are
shown, one of six acres, situated in Beggars Bush Lane and worked
by James Shaw Hellier, the other of two acres in Townsend Close
and cultivated by John Cartwright.

A group of old cottages, now known as Nailers Row, in Giggetty Lane.

Nailing is mentioned in the tithe document in two ways, both as nail 'warehouses' (four) and three as 'nailers' shops'. The warehouses would have been the centre of the domestic production or 'putting-out' system used extensively in the nail-making industry. Iron bars would have been stored in them until a nailer collected them to turn into nails in his workshop. Then the nails and any spare iron bars would be returned by the workman and he would be paid for the finished product. The nails would be stored at the warehouse until they were sold on. Two of the 'shops' are small (see Table 6) and are part of a complex of buildings which include pigsties and stables as well as houses. This probably indicates that they were originally farm buildings which were converted to nailers' 'workshops'. The third 'shop', in a row of houses, is of a similar size to the other houses, indicating that a domestic house was converted to a 'workshop'. Perhaps a room in the house had been converted into a workshop and the occupier either employed nailers to work on his behalf, or rented out the space to nailers.

The Tithe Commutation Act was part of the movement to both reform and preserve during the nineteenth century. The reform was to remove often medieval restrictions or practices that hindered or prevented economic or social progress. The act removed many of the obvious criticisms the Church of England faced, especially from radicals, Non-conformists and Catholics. It moved to a standard rate across the country, and it removed the need to consider payment 'in kind'. The resulting 'tithe rent charge' did not vary depending upon the use or improvement of the land, so it could not be presented as a 'tax on progress'.[8] However, as this short chapter has shown, there is much more that can be learnt about Wombourne from the information the commissioners gathered.

Table 6: Details of properties identified as used in nail-making

Property Type	Size (acres)	Owner	Occupier	Location
Warehouse	0.019	John Davies	John Elwell	On Common Road, opposite Walk Lane Farm
Warehouse	0.013	Maria Hill	Jane Johnson	On the corner between High Street and Gravel Hill
Warehouse	0.013	Maria Hill	David Wilkes	On the corner between High Street and Gravel Hill
Warehouse	0.013	Thomas Jones	Thomas Jones	On Rookery Road
Nailer's shop	0.004	John Davies	Benjamin Corns	In a side road off High Street, approximately where Walker's Way now exists
Nailer's shop	0.003	Percy Edward	John York	In a side road off High Street, approximately where Walker's Way now exists
Nailer's shop	0.013	William York	Thomas Moseley	On the corner between Church Road and Windmill Bank

Notes

1. D. M. Stenton, *English Society in the Early Middle Ages* (Pelican, 1964)
2. The National Archives: 'The history of tithes' (#18160)
3. D. M. Stenton, *op. sit.*, p. 207
4. H. P. R. Finberg, *The Formation of England 550–1042* (Paladin, 1976), p. 202
5. *Victoria County History of Staffordshire*, quoting Valor Eccl.iii 243
6. *Ibid.*
7. The National Archives: Tithe Commutation from 1836 (#18162)
8. A. W. Purdue, 'An Oxford College, Two Parishes and a Tithe Farmer: The Modernisation of Tithe Collection', *Rural History*, vol. 8 (1997), pp. 1–19 (p. 15)

Religious Houses

David Banks

St Benedict Biscop

It is thought that the first church was a Saxon one built in AD 910. This would have been of simple wattle and daub and hence no evidence of its existence remains. It may have been built to pray for the souls of those who died at the Battle of Tettenhall, when King Edward the Elder defeated the Danes.

Other accounts suggest that the Church of St Benedict Biscop existed about AD 1086. Certainly the Domesday Book indicates the presence of a priest then. Benedict Biscop was an Anglo-Saxon abbot

of *c.*628–90 who founded Monkwearmouth-Jarrow Priory. He was considered to be a saint after his death. This was the only known church dedicated to him until 2005, when a new church in Jarrow was given the same dedication.

In 1150 the church was given by Guido de Olphini, lord of the manor, to the Cluniac Priory of St James at Dudley.

In medieval times the church would have been of sandstone. Certainly in the fourteenth century it would have consisted of a nave, a three-bay north aisle, a chancel and a spire.

Over the next few centuries various modifications were made to the church. In 1639 a porch and a gate were added. By 1736 west and north galleries with family pews had been built by Edwin Sherwin. In 1767 an organ was added and in 1782–3 a new north gallery and vestry room in the spire were built.

However, with the growth in population of Wombourne, the church had become too small by the 1840s for local Christians. So an architect, George Street, was employed to design a bigger church. It was largely rebuilt in thirteenth-century style. All except the tower and the walls of the north aisle and north transept were torn down. The new parts were the chancel, organ chamber, south aisle and the south porch. The spire was partially taken down and rebuilt four feet higher with a new cross and vane on the top. Over the next 150 years a lady chapel and extended vestry were built. So the present church consists of several styles:

1. The south aisle with lancet windows in early English style
2. The chancel has thirteenth-century windows
3. The north aisle with perpendicular windows reminiscent of Reformation style.

Protestant Nonconformity

The Dissenters were members of a religious body separated from the established Church. They were mainly opposed to state interference in religious matters and formed their own Churches. The Act of Uniformity wanted Anglican ordination for all clergy. Those opposed became Nonconformists.

There is plenty of evidence for Dissenters in Wombourne:

> In 1672 Ithell Bates's house at Orton was licensed for Congregationalist worship
> In 1720 dissenting meetings were served by itinerant preachers
> In 1778 Jacob Cartwright's house was registered for Protestant Dissenters
> By 1825 50 years of Protestant Dissenters had failed

The United Reformed Church in High Street, originally built as the
Congregational Church.

In 1813 Congregationalist services and occasional preach-
ings were held at Mr and Mrs Stephen's house. Later this was
moved to Windmill Bank and then Mill Lane
In 1835 a barn at Lower End, which is on the corner of Gravel
Hill and Rookery Road used as a day school, was taken over
for Sunday worship and a Sunday school was started
In 1851 the United Reform chapel in Mill Lane was opened.
Later a vestry and a schoolroom were added in 1870 and
enlarged in 1925. In 1951 they had a resident minister.

Roman Catholicism

Recusants are people who refused to attend Anglican services and
largely remained Roman Catholic, keeping to the faith that existed
before Henry VIII's reforms. Some recusants are mentioned before
the early eighteenth century:

> Edward Powell and his wife in 1665
> Thomas Wheeler and his wife Eleanor in 1670
> Elizabeth Banton and her three daughters in 1706, the only
> papists at that time.

St Bernadette's Roman Catholic Church, Rennison Drive.

In 1952 Mass was said every Sunday in the British Legion Hall in Maypole Street by a priest from St Michael's, Merry Hill. In 1961 St Bernadette's Church was built in Rennison Drive. It was designed by C. V. Mason of Mason, Richards & Partner of Wolverhampton. It is of brick with a thin fibreglass spire. It appointed a resident priest in 1962, who lived in Giggetty Lane until a presbytery was built adjoining the church in 1965.

Methodists

Wesleyan Methodists were worshipping in Common Lane at the cottage of Samuel Evans in 1829.

In 1850 a chapel was built where Chapel Street is now. Then in 1894 a new and larger chapel was built in Common Lane. In 1966 a schoolroom was built as a two-storeyed building, with more extensions in 1960 when the church was remodelled.

In 1851 there was Primitive Methodist preaching in Grettons Row off School Road.

In Smestow services were held in a cottage in Chapel Lane in 1860. A hall for Sunday school was added. However, in 1973 the chapel and school were closed.

Methodist Chapel, Common Road.

The King's Way Church Centre.

Other Religious Activities

Some evidence for other religious activities is known:

> In 1851 a non-denominational group held meetings every Sunday evening in a house in Wombourne.

> In 1924 an International Bible Students' Association registered an assembly room in Planks Lane, but this was cancelled in 1928.

Venerable Bede

A mission room belonging to the parish church was opened in 1890 in Chapel Street. This was replaced by the Mission Church of the Venerable Bede in Giggetty Lane in 1957, again to serve the expanding parish. It was designed by B. A. Miller of Liverpool. This is a sister church of Benedict Biscop. Both churches are Anglican.

The church derives its name from Bede the Venerable, who was a religious writer and historian based in the locality of County Durham. He lived from 673 to 735. He was also a monk at the sister monasteries of Monkwearmouth and Jarrow and his first abbot was Benedict Biscop!

Church of the Venerable Bede, Giggetty Lane.

The Staffordshire and Worcestershire Canal

Philip Pennell

The birth certificate, as it were, for this navigable cut or canal was the Act of Parliament which granted to the Company of Proprietors of the Staffordshire and Worcestershire Canal Navigation to build a canal from the River Severn between Bewdley and Titton Brook, in the County of Worcester, to cross the River Trent, near Haywood Mill, in the County of Stafford, and to communicate with a canal intended to be made between the said River Trent and the River Mersey. The act was passed on 14 May 1766. It also empowered the company to raise sufficient money to enable work to begin almost immediately. This was no problem as the merchants of Wolverhampton had met some three months previously and backed the scheme. It is obvious from the title of the act that there had been much preliminary work on the route. Indeed, Brindley, the engineer in charge of the project, was in the area in February 1766 at the request of Stourbridge merchants, discussing the line of a cut from that town to the River Severn. Nevertheless it was not until 1768 that work began on the ground and 1772 when the whole of 46 miles was officially opened. However, the canal was used in parts before that, linking Stourport with Wolverhampton by the turn of the decade. Thus by 1780 Wombourne was using the canal for transporting goods southwards. About the same time the Stourbridge Canal (which joins the Staffordshire and Worcestershire at Stewponey) was completed and thus the south-west of the Black County was connected to the south-west of England and especially Bristol from where goods made locally were exported.

The reason that the canal passed through Wombourne is that it was designed by Brindley. He has often been described as the constructor of winding navigations lacking major engineering works and adhering to the contours of the land.[1] So it was obvious to him that the southern part of the canal should follow the River Stour and its

STAFFORD

Stoke-on-Trent

Trent and Mersey Canal

Great Haywood Junction

Rugeley

STAFFORDSHIRE AND WORCESTERSHIRE CANAL
46 Miles and 43 Locks from Stourport Basins To Great Haywood Junction

PENKRIDGE

Staffordshire And Worcestershire Canal

Hatherton Canal

Market Drayton

Shropshire Union Canal

Aldersley Junction

Autherley Junction

BCN Main Line

Birmingham

WOLVERHAMPTON

WOMBOURNE

Staffordshire And Worcestershire Canal

Stourton Junction

KINVER

Stourbridge Canal

Brierley Hill

Town Arm

STOURBRIDGE

KIDDERMINSTER

Bewdley

River Severn

0 1 2 3 miles

STOURPORT-ON-SEVERN

Stourport Basins

Worcester

A section of the Staffordshire and Worcestershire Canal.

tributary, the Smestow Brook, and the northern should follow the River Penk to the River Trent. Within these broad parameters the line of the cut would be decided by physical features, landowner- ship and proximity to materials and goods requiring transport, all of which favoured a route which passed near to the village. But the village did not have any canal-side industry following the building of the canal, unlike Swindon where the existing iron mill transferred its water-borne transport from the river to the canal and used it until the middle of the twentieth century when the ironworks closed. However, it did have several wharfs where goods from the local- ity were loaded onto barges for onward transport mainly to Bristol and the south-west, with Wombourne contributing sand from Brick- bridge and other quarries. Other goods using the Wombourne wharfs were coal for the waterworks' pumps and, before the Stourbridge Canal took over, pot clay from Amblecote and bricks. Thus Wom- bourne became an entrepôt for the south-west of the Black Coun- try. The canal was extremely successful for the first forty years of its life, but from 1815 onwards the Dudley Canal linking to the Bir- mingham Canal and then to the Worcester Canal, then joining the River Severn, proved more attractive especially for the carrying of coal. These circumstances forced the company to extend the hours the locks could be used, until they were available 24 hours a day by 1830.[2] Then the Birmingham and Liverpool Junction Canal Com- pany took much of the traffic from the northern section of the canal and a toll war began, which affected the amount of traffic on the Staf- fordshire and Worcestershire Canal.

Despite this competition between canal companies and the later competition from the railways the company continued to make prof- its yearly during the nineteenth century although these fell in value from the 1860s.

Nevertheless it was still profitable throughout its life until the canals were nationalised in 1948. This was mainly due, in the latter years, to the transportation of coal from the Cannock coalfield to the Stourport power station. However in 1949 the government came to the conclusion that the canal was not a commercial proposition and threatened to close it, which led to the opposition forming itself into the Staffordshire and Worcestershire Canal Society, whose efforts were successful in preventing the closure and getting the canal reclassified as a 'cruiseway' in 1968.[3] Thus it has had a second life as a recreation facility for the past 45 years.

However, despite the fact that the canal is situated in the village there has not been a symbiotic relationship of note between them in the period of canal's existence, rather a number of isolated and minor instances. Firstly there were the two staircases of locks, one at Bot- terham which is a normal design, the other the unique one at Bratch,

This aerial view shows the canal running from L to R at the bottom of the picture.

Bratch lock.

which were the first two constructed in England. Then there are the quays, which are mentioned above, and the influence the canal had on the number of pubs in the village, including two which are no longer there: the Navigation, which was situated diagonally opposite the Round Oak and the Boat at Botterham, and one which was built to catch the trade generated by the quay off Bridgnorth Road appropriately called the Waggon and Horses. Indeed in its recreation era, the canal did not call on Wombourne as much as the settlements to the south of it, e.g. Hinksford has far more canal-side moorings, and Ashwood has a marina whereas the village has only a few moorings at the Bratch.

The Boat Inn at Botterham.

Notes

1. Ray Shill, *Silent Highways*, Stroud, The History Press, 2011
2. *et seq*. Staffordshire and Worcestershire Canal KinverOnline.co.uk
3. Staffordshire and Worcestershire Canal Society Homepage

Schools In Wombourne: *A Brief Perspective on the Educational System*

Marian Innes

The History of Education in England

The history of education in England can be traced back to the Roman occupation. However, over the centuries the structure of the educational system has had to adapt in order to meet the requirements imposed by changing legislation, and economic and educational needs.

Education in the nineteenth century tended to be the preserve of the rich as it had to be paid for. However the elementary schools which also existed during this period charged only a few pence and were deliberately intended to provide a basic education for the poor.

The most highly educated were those who worked in the Church or were attached to a religious organisation and able to access a school attached to a cathedral or monastery. These schools taught Latin – the language of the Church – to future priests and monks. They were the forerunners of the grammar school and have their origins in Saxon ecclesiastical establishments.

Many grammar schools date from the 1550s, a period when new foundations were endowed to replace those lost at the Reformation. By the seventeenth century boarding and day grammar schools existed. Endowments provided free, or almost free, education and the terms and conditions of such endowments usually prevented any deviation from classical studies. Over time, however, the curriculum was broadened, first to include ancient Greek and later English and other European languages, mathematics, history and geography and other subjects.

In 1840 the Grammar Schools Act expanded the curriculum to include science and literature. In the late Victoria era, grammar schools were reorganised to provide secondary education and became the selective tier of state-funded secondary education from the mid

1940s through to the late 1960s when non-selective comprehensive education was introduced. Some grammar schools became fully independent at this time, charged fees and retained 'grammar' in their name. However, the majority were abolished or became comprehensive.

The public school system derived originally from grammar schools. They became known as 'public' because of their ability to attract pupils from outside their own locality. The rejuvenation of public schools in the second half of the nineteenth century encouraged the establishment of preparatory schools in which pupils could be prepared for grammar school admission. About a third of today's public schools originated from grammar schools founded between the fourteenth and seventeenth centuries.[1]

In the eighteenth century schools of industry were set up to provide the poor with manual training and elementary instruction. Such a school was opened at Kendal in the Lake District in 1799 and, according to the records of the Society for Bettering the Condition of the Poor (III.300–312), children were taught reading, writing, geography and religion. At the school older girls were employed in knitting, sewing, spinning and housework while the younger girls participated in knitting only. Older boys were taught shoemaking and younger ones prepared machinery for carding wool.

The early 1800s also saw the formation of British schools. Joseph Lancaster, a Quaker, founded the Royal Lancastrian Society, later renamed the British and Foreign School Society. A feature of the society was the use of a monitoring system whereby older children taught younger ones under the supervision of staff. This method was copied by other types of schools including those which were later part of the state system. The curriculum provided at that time tended to be similar to that of the schools of industry and included reading, writing and arithmetic plus practical activities such as cobbling, tailoring, gardening, simple agricultural operations for boys and spinning, sewing, knitting, lace-making and baking for girls.[2]

During this period ragged schools developed from the work of John Pounds, a cobbler in Portsmouth, who from 1818 provided free schooling for the very poorest children. Later in 1844 Lord Shaftesbury helped organise an official union of ragged schools and by 1869 there were about 200. Other schools in existence were common day schools which provided private, low-fee, elementary education as did dame schools, charity schools or informal village schools. All of these were usually run by schoolmistresses teaching the three Rs (reading, (w)riting and (a)rithmetic). Sometimes individuals bestowed a chantry, an endowment to cover expenses for the saying of prayers for the soul of the bestower, and occasionally a chantry school grew from such bequests.

District schools catered for the education of children in work-houses, while national schools under the auspices of the National Society for the Education of the Poor (formed in 1811) took over other schools already established by the Society for Promoting Christian Knowledge, which had been founded in 1698. These schools provided education for the industrial poor, insisting on subordination, frugality and gratitude. They were supported by voluntary subscription. In 1824 Parliament made a grant of £24,000 to elementary schools which was shared between the British and national schools. By 1851 the National Society controlled over 17,000 schools.

England's industrial revolution, which had begun in the second half of the eighteenth century, introduced new agricultural techniques that freed workers from the land and resulted in large numbers of the population moving to the new industrial cities, attracted by the construction of factories for the mass production of goods. It also resulted in low wages, slum housing and the use of child labour.

Peel's Factory Act of 1802 was introduced to preserve the health of apprentices, many of whom were young pauper children, brought in from workhouses to be employed in cotton mills and other factories. The act required an employer to provide instruction in reading, writing and arithmetic, and such instruction was to be part of the 12-hour working day which usually began at 6 a.m. and ended at 9 p.m. A further act in 1833 also made attendance at factory schools a condition of employment for juveniles and within 10 years approximately 40% of children in the manufacturing areas were attending.

The act also stipulated the maximum number of hours children could work in a day, i.e. for children from 9–12 years of age, a maximum of nine hours per day; and children aged 13–18 years of age, a maximum of twelve hours per day. All children were to have at least two hours of schooling per day. By 1901 the minimum working age had been raised to 12 years. A further act in 1937 stated that under-16s were to work no more than a 44-hour week and those between 16 and 18 years no more than 48 hours per week.

This type of work had already been pioneered by employers such as Robert Owen (1771–1858) who established the first infant school in New Lanark, Scotland in 1816. Children were admitted at the age of two and cared for while their parents worked in the local mills. Infant schools were at first partly 'minding schools' for young children in industrial areas but they also endeavoured to promote the children's physical well-being while at the same time offering opportunities for their moral and social training as well as providing some elementary instruction in the three Rs.

Other legislation at this time included the Poor Law Act of 1844 which ensured that teachers were appointed for workhouse children, leading to the formation of district schools. The Industrial Schools Act of 1857 empowered magistrates to send children to school to learn a trade. The introduction of the Elementary Education Act 1870, commonly known as Forster's Education Act, since it was devised by William Edward Forster, created the concept of compulsory education for children up to ten years of age. At that age a child could obtain a certificate and leave but if too few attendances had been registered then that child had to stay on until 13 years of age.[3]

For poorer families this proved difficult, as it was more lucrative to send them to work if the opportunity to do so arose. Attendance officers would visit the homes of children who failed to attend school, though this often proved to be ineffective. A report commissioned in 1941 and published in 1943, which related to the employment of young people employed in the Staffordshire Potteries at this time found that children began work as early as three or four years of age and regular employment tended to commence between seven and eight years of age. A large proportion of those employed were orphans, children of widows or children who belonged to the very poorest families. The report also found that in many of the trades, especially in pin-making, nail-making, lace-making and others, children

> *did not have sufficient food, nor warm and decent clothing; many of them were clothed in rags and this prevented them from attending Sunday school for want of proper clothing.*

Extracts relating to records of children working in the Staffordshire Potteries give an indication of poverty levels and working conditions at that time.[4]

> *Log No. 1 – Child aged 12 years: 'I have worked in the Press Room for 2 years. I come in at 6.30 in the morning and leave at 6.00 at night. I get 4 shillings* [a shilling is a former British coin with a monetary value equal to 1/20 of a pound or 12 pence] *a week. I give my money to my Mother. I have no Father, he was a Presser working here too but he died of consumption at 44 years of age. It is hot in the Press Room and cold when I go outside. Makes no difference to the clothes I wear – summer or winter.'*

> *Log No. 7 – child aged 9 years: 'I work in the oven as a Stoker and carry coal to the fires. I begin at 6.00 am and leave at 5.00 pm. I don't know how much wages I get – all goes to my Father. He sometimes gives me 1d* [one old penny – a former British coin with a monetary value equal to 1/12 of a shilling and 240th of a pound]. *I can't read or write.'*

> *Log No. 14 – child aged 13 years: 'I worked in the dipping-house for 12 months. My mother has 10 of us to support, my Father often gets drunk; can't read nor write; don't go to Sunday school or Day school; don't know why except that Mother is so poor and haven't got no clothes.'*

> *Log No. 47 – child aged 13 years: 'I have been employed here for 3 years. I am what is called a turn-wheel engine thrower. I come in at 6.30, go at 6. Can't*

read or write. I get 2 shillings a week. Give my money to my Mother. I once got hurt; had my hand nigh clean off; could not work for 6 months. I clean by hand, all the little wheels, when it is going sometimes. The machinery is not fenced off.'

In areas where educational provision was problematic, elected school boards were set up. These boards could create local by-laws, stipulating required attendance and had the power to fine the parents of those children who did not attend. Exceptions were made for chronic illness, long distance, or on proof (certification) of a child having reached the required standard of education as set down by the board. The Technical Institutes Act allowed county councils to levy a rate of 1d to provide technical education. In 1893 and 1899 the school-leaving age was raised to 11 and then to 12 respectively.[5] In 1891 elementary education was made free.

The development of the educational system described was established by individuals and groups who believed and campaigned for mass education. However, it is worthy of note that hostility to the idea of educating the poor existed, e.g. when the Parochial Schools Bill of 1807 was debated in the Commons, Conservative MP Davies Giddy warned that

giving education to the labouring classes would, in effect, be found to be prejudicial to their morals and happiness; it would teach them to despise their lot in life, instead of making them good servants in agriculture and other laborious employments to which their rank in society had destined them and would burden the country with enormous and incalculable expense.[6]

Local history sources from the late seventeenth century taken from school logs indicate conditions prevailing at the time.[7] They include:

School log, February, 1875 – Two girls expelled from school as they have several times refused to take their turn at dinner time to sweep up the hearth and dust the room and have tried several times to influence the other children to be disobedient.

School log, 17 July, 1875 – The attendance still very low most likely the consequence of the haymaking. The children being kept at home to convey the parents' meals or look after the younger children.

School log, 17 January, 1881 – The fire had only been made for half an hour, the ink was frozen in the well. To clean the slates was impossible for if one was wet it was covered with ice before it dried.

School log, 21 February, 1881 – The attendance was very low on account of the severe weather. The children were supplied with warm soup from the vicarage.

At this time killer diseases such as smallpox, dysentery, consumption and typhus were widespread. Even if an illness was survived, there could be permanent and severe consequences: for instance, scarlet fever left many children blind and deaf. A shortage of food, inadequate housing and lack of access to medical care and medication all had disastrous effects, especially on the poorer classes as information extracted from a further school log dated October 1874 indicates:

> *Between 12 and 16 October – 2 children dead. On 19 October very few children were present – 12 absent through illness – diphtheria. By 24 October 2 more children dead. Orders given to close the school. Re-opened on 2 November – discovered 2 more children had died.*

In the early 1900s the Women's Institute, recognising the benefits of recording life as it was in Staffordshire at that time, collated a diverse store of memories from members highlighting aspects of life in a number of areas.[8] Some of those memories drew attention to the fact that corporal punishment was perceived as part of the educative process and was often viewed as 'character building', e.g. *'to go to school we had to walk 2 miles through fields and climb a stile. We were the only children excused dirty boots – the others had to line up for the cane across the hand by the headteacher.'*

The use of the cane can be further evidenced as far back as 1860 when William Cox, a headmaster at Bobbington School, was dismissed after complaints about his excessive discipline. It was not until after the 1967 Plowden Report, *Children and their Primary Schools*, that the abolition of corporal punishment in state schools was treated as a major issue. In 1986 it was outlawed in state schools, but it was not until 1998 that it was abolished altogether in the remaining independent schools in existence at that time.

The change process continued in the twentieth century with the Balfour Education Act of 1902 empowering local authorities to provide both elementary and secondary education.[9] Secondary education provision stipulated that boys attended state grammar schools and girls high schools. The later Fisher Education Act of 1918 made secondary education compulsory up to the age of 14 and also devolved responsibility to the state. The 1944 Education Act abolished fees in state secondary schools and elementary education was reorganised into infant and junior schools.[10] It raised the school-leaving age to 15 and established the tripartite system whereby secondary education was graded into grammar, secondary modern and technical schools.

In the post-war years the tripartite system became controversial. Its critics condemned it as being elitist while its defenders claimed that it allowed pupils to obtain a good education through merit as opposed to family income. The Labour Government in 1965 formulated proposals

The Wombourn Institute, completed in 1833 and now known as 'the Hand in Hand', with the spire of the parish church behind.

to move away from selection at 11 and replace this with comprehensive schooling. This was done by means of Circular 10/65 and the withholding of funding from any school that sought to retain selection.[11] Subsequently the school-leaving age was raised to 16 in 1972.

Following the general election of 1979 the Conservative Party regained power and introduced the New Vocationalism spearheaded by a Youth Opportunities Programme for all 16–18-year-olds. This ran until 1983 when it was replaced by the Youth Training Scheme. In 1986 National Qualifications were introduced to revitalise vocational training.

The Education Reform Act of 1988 introduced a National Curriculum making it compulsory for schools to teach specific subjects and syllabuses. Assessments were introduced at key stages, that is, at 7, 11, 14 and 16 years of age. League tables showing performance statistics for each school were published in newspapers and on the internet.[12] Formula funding was introduced, as was open enrolment and choice for parents. Schools could, if they so wished, opt out of government control and become grant-maintained schools receiving funding direct from central government.

In 1994 Modern Apprenticeships encompassing knowledge- and competency-based elements, as well as the key skills of literacy and numeracy were initiated. Following the 1997 General Election, in which Labour returned to power, further changes were implemented. These included the tailoring of education to each child's ability, abolishing the grant-maintained status and giving schools the choice of rejoining the local authority as maintained community schools or becoming foundation schools.

In the twenty-first century, education in England is overseen by the Department for Business, Innovation and Skills, and local authorities have responsibility for implementing policy for public and state schools at a local level. The system is divided into early years (ages 3–4), primary education (ages 4–11), secondary education (ages 11–18) and tertiary education (age 18+).

Full-time education is compulsory for all children with the Education and Skills Act of 2008 stipulating attendance between the ages of five and 17 (from 2013) and up to 18 (from 2015).[13] State-run schools are financed through national taxation and, while education is free, schools may charge pupils for extra-curricular activities, e.g. swimming, field trips etc. England also has a tradition of independent schooling and parents may choose to educate their children by other suitable means such as Elective Home Education.[14]

At present there are six main types of schools in England:[15]

> Community schools (formerly county schools)
> Voluntary Controlled schools – nearly always church schools
> Voluntary Aided schools – linked to Church or other non-denominational organisations
> Foundation schools – whereby a governing body has overall responsibility
> Academy schools – established by the 1997–2010 Labour government
> Free schools – introduced by the Conservative-Liberal Democrat coalition following the 2010 general election

There are also a number of city technology colleges and academies which are secondary schools funded and monitored by the Department

of Education. Academies can also accept funding from private sources such as individuals or companies.

All state-funded schools are inspected by the Office for Standards in Education which publishes reports on the quality of education on individual schools on a regular basis. Schools judged to be providing an inadequate standard of education may be subject to special measures which may include replacing the governing body or senior staff.

Schools in Wombourne[16]

The school system has developed over the centuries and Wombourne, as a village, has adapted to meet the needs of its inhabitants. In Wombourne schools have been in existence since the early seventeenth century; the earliest was opened by the curate of the parish church, Nathaniel Smart, in 1638. In 1766, Sir Samuel Hellier and a group of parishioners founded a charity school for 20 children supported by subscriptions from the parishioners. The school was at work by 1767 but was eventually closed in 1770 as a result of disputes between Sir Hellier and the parishioners.

A Sunday school was later opened in 1805, following in the tradition of the first Sunday school, which appears to have been founded in Catterick, Yorkshire in 1763. Sunday schools taught the poor – both children and adults – and had a focus on Bible reading, as opposed to the three Rs, which were considered 'less necessary'. The Sunday School Movement derived its success from Robert Raikes who founded a school in Gloucester in 1780, employed four women to teach and charged 1d a week. The movement started with a school for boys in the slums. The best available time was on Sunday as the boys were often working in factories on the other six days. By 1785 the movement was growing in popularity and a society was formed for the establishment and support of Sunday schools throughout the country. The Sunday School Union was later founded in 1803 to improve schools in the London area.

Subsequently, demand locally for a more comprehensive education led to a National School being built in 1833 situated west of Wombourne church. This was financed by Sarah Dalton of the Lloyd in Penn. In 1835 the school had a mistress; a master was appointed in 1841. By the mid 1840s there was an average attendance of 49 boys and 52 girls. An infants' school was opened in part of the almshouses in the early 1850s.

In the 1880s there were four day schools in Wombourne teaching 40 boys and 51 girls. The first day school was opened in 1821, a second in 1828. Two private schools had also been established. One was run by Thomas Hill and held in a barn at the corner of Gravel Hill and Rookery Road. The other was a dame school started in 1851 by Elizabeth Pilsbury and situated in Upper Street (the present Church Street). The usual fee was 3d or 4d per week. A night school run by the Wombourne Mutual Improvement Society was held at the national school twice a week during the winter of 1863–4, with each student paying 1d an evening. It ceased the following winter because of poor attendance.

The National School was rebuilt in 1860 at a cost of £1,400 on land from the glebe on the north side of School Road. It was financed by government and National Society grants with the remaining finance coming from subscriptions. The school was staffed by a master and a mistress (husband and wife) and infants' mistress. The school was supported by a levy of 2d and 6d with the higher rate being paid by those in the upper classes where more advanced subjects were taught. By 1869/70 the school was receiving a government grant.

Old Church School Demolished

The Demolition Men moved into School Road in November and within two weeks the old Church School building, which has served generations of Wombourne schoolchildren for over a century, was no more.

At this time there was an average attendance of 116 pupils which increased to 185 pupils by the mid 1880s and by 1905 had an attendance of 311. A new school building was officially opened in 1974 and the old school demolished. In the late 1970s, average attendance at the school, by then St Benedict Biscop Church of England Controlled First School, was 213.

Although the need for a school in Swindon was recognised in the 1840s it was not until 1864 that a school was built south of St John's Church. This was supported by subscription and school pence, i.e. children paid 4d, 2d or 1d a week, the rate being determined by their parents' income and the number of children attending from any one family. The school received a government grant in 1872. Average attendance in 1867 was 56, in 1884 it was 53 and in 1892 it was 95. The school eventually moved to new premises in Wombourne Road in 1968 and by the 1970s average attendance at what was then St John's Church of England Controlled Primary School was 115.

Wombourne was not alone in ensuring that its young people benefited from an education. The neighbouring parishes of Bobbington and Trysull also did their bit. Records indicate that a school was established in Bobbington in 1792. This was run by Hannah and Mary Corbett and catered for 20 boys and 12 girls aged between 8 and 15 years of age. In 1891 average attendance was 17 boys and 28 girls and school fees were 2d and 3d for those who could afford them. A dame school existed in the 1840s and a Sunday school was established in 1845. In the latter part of the nineteenth century there was a private school run by a Mrs Gretton and called the Marigolds, at Broadfields Farm to the south of the village. By 1860 William Cox had established a private school. This was taken over in 1872 by Elizabeth Cox and the tradition was subsequently continued by another relative, J. Cox, from premises at Bobbington House Farm.

In Trysull there was a schoolmaster teaching boys in the late 1680s. In 1707 the school was endowed with land at Trimpley in Kidderminster with £200 given by Thomas Rudge of Westminster for the purposes of teaching the poor children of the parish. A Sunday school existed by 1817. In 1843 a new school was built on the east side of Trysull Green on the site of the former poorhouse. In the late 1840s there were 21 boys and 18 girls at the school and in 1864 there were 16 free pupils as well as 10 boys, 27 girls and 18 infants paying 2d a week and one boy and girl who were taught writing and paid 4d. Average attendance by the mid 1870s was 85. In 1895 the school had to be abandoned after storm damage and a new school was opened on the north side of the Green in 1896 with a bequest of £3,000 donated by Eliza Baker of Bromsgrove. In 1833 there were three private schools teaching 28 boys and 31 girls.

Although Wombourne is designated as a village, it has expanded in the years since World War II and school attendance figures have also increased accordingly. In 2013 numbers of children attending include 1200 pupils at Ounsdale High School, 451 at Westfield Community Primary School, 264 pupils at Blakeley Heath Primary School, 250 at St Benedict Biscop Church of England Primary School, 76 pupils at St Bernadette's Catholic Primary School and 32 at Cherry Trees School.[17]

Pre-school education is provided by voluntary playgroups and private day nurseries in addition to the nursery classes provided at the four primary schools in the village. Cherry Trees Special School takes children between the ages of two and 11. From the age of 11 children attend Ounsdale High School. Adult education classes are held at the Community Centre and at Ounsdale School. Wombourne Leisure Centre, based at Ounsdale High School, has a large swimming pool, used jointly by local schools.

Considerable changes over the years have influenced the way the educational system has evolved. The advent of new technology, the internet and variations in the way information is accessed will ensure that change continues to occur.

Picture by Computer Weekly

THEY ARE THE CHAMPIONS

Congratulations to our team from Ounsdale School, whose computer project has won them a DEC Classic minicomputer, a year's maintenance, and a training Course, worth in all a total of over £9,000. The School won the close fought final in the Win-a-Computer competition sponsored by Computer Weekly and Digital Equipment. 'Ounsdale' project, a network analysis technique for application to shortest route problems, was judged best after a close, exciting final held at the Waldorf Hotel, London, on Tuesday, 27th May.

the station the steadying influence of Mr. Black-ford, experience of life teaches one to approach

all situations with cau-tion, reassured the team that whatever the out-come, the experience would be invaluable to them. During the Com-*Contd. on Page 2*

Your property

Notes

1. John Richardson, *The Local Historian's Encyclopedia*. 3rd edn (London, Historical Publications, 2003)
2. Derek Gillard, 'Education in England: a brief history' (www.educationengland.org.uk/history, 2011)
3. School Resources (http://www.genuki.org.uk)
4. Report commissioned to look at the employment of children in the Staffordshire Potteries (1841). C.199/72. Wombourne History Room
5. http://www.dfes.gov.uk/schoolattendance
6. *Hansard*, vol. 9, col. 798, 13 July 1807
7. Staffordshire County Council Education Department, 'Elementary Education in Staffordshire', Local History Source Book no. 7, C.199/23
8. Staffordshire Federation of Women's Institutes, 'Within Living Memory: Childhood and Schooldays' (1992), Wombourne History Room C.242
9. G. R. Searle, *A New England? Peace and War, 1886–1918* (Clarendon Press, 2005)
10. School-leaving age brief (www.politics.co.uk)
11. A. Sampson, *The Changing Anatomy of Britain* (London, Hodder & Stoughton, 1982)
12. School achievement and attainment tables (http://www.dfes.gov.uk/performancetables)
13. Education and Skills Act 2008 (Office of Public Sector Information)
14. 'Elective Home Education: Guidelines for Local Authorities', Dept. for Children, Schools and Families (2007)

15. Categories of schools – overview
    (http://www.governornet.co.uk/cropArticle.cfm)
16. Unless otherwise stated the following section is based (with the kind permission of the present county editor) on the schools' sections of the 'History of Wombourne, Bobbington and Trysull' in the *Victoria County History of Staffordshire* (1984), pp. 64–76 and 185–224 giving full references
17. Numbers based on information obtained from School PEL

Industry

David Taylor

The history of industry, or economic activity, in Wombourne could be called the story of change itself: from, imperceptible beginnings, but steadily gaining momentum and size until, some would say, reaching near-breakneck speed in the last 100 years. Many aspects of that story mirrors what has happened in the wider English and then British economy, while some are unique to the specific conditions of Wombourne, its geography and geology. As Halford Mackinder maintained in 1904, geography is of prime importance in determining politics and economics.[1]

In the Domesday Book, Wombourne, Orton and Chasepool are mentioned, having a priest, villagers, smallholders and slaves, as well as various ploughs and two mills. Most of the land must have been arable, but eight acres of meadow are recorded in Orton and Wombourne, whilst Chasepool, which is in the King's Forest, is described as waste, meaning open common land.[2] In common with much of England the predominant source of employment for the following centuries would have been agriculture, with some localised domestic industrial activity. Iron production and working would have been small scale and dependent upon ease of access to the primary raw materials. Wombourne is close to, but not on, easily available outcrops of iron ore, limestone and coal. Prior to the development in the eighteenth century of techniques that allowed quality iron-working with coal, charcoal was the primary source of energy, but Wombourne had little woodland suitable for charcoal production. Therefore industrial activities were concentrated in the parishes to the north and east of Wombourne, where the requisite raw materials were more easily available. However, there are indications that there was some industrial activity in Wombourne parish from the seventeenth century. Forges are mentioned by Dud Dudley in 1621 at Greensforge, Heath Forge and Swin (or Swindon), although there is some doubt about the accuracy of his claims. It is known that a

Charles Cornwallis leased a hammer mill in Wombourne from John Dudley in 1602, which appears to have been converted from a corn mill.[3] A hammer mill uses water power to operate a large hammer to beat iron bars into thin strips. These strips could then be cut into objects such as nails, sometimes at a blade mill with a water-operated saw. There is a mention of a blade mill at Wombourne in 1691.[4]

Towards the end of the seventeenth century and into the eighteenth century there are records of forges and mills in the parish being supplied with pig iron from furnaces elsewhere in South Staffordshire. The Swin Forge in Swindon was recorded in 1736 to be producing 100 tons per annum, whilst in 1750 it was recorded as producing 140 tons per annum. This might indicate that it had changed from a forge to a full furnace. However, manufacturing, as represented by nailing, developed as an overspill from Dudley and Sedgley, areas more favoured for the production of iron and its working into objects such as nails, tools and buckles. Nash estimated that there were 34,000 nailers at work around Dudley.[5] However, between 1681 and 1720 only six are identifiable in Wombourne according to probate inventories,[6] but in the eighteenth century the number grew for a variety of reasons. The development of industry in towns increased wage rates there, assisted by the ease with which guilds and other bodies could regulate wage rates in relatively concentrated areas. Rural workers were cheaper to employ because, in rural parishes such as

The Bratch Pumping Station completed in 1905.

Wombourne, a dual economy existed: workers would spend some time working in agriculture; they might also occupy some 'waste' ground to raise livestock and undertake domestic industrial work. Nail-making was an ideal activity for this type of latter occupation. The 'putting-out' system, in which middlemen distributed iron bars to be made into nails which they then collected and marketed as far afield as London and the overseas colonies, provided working capital and the organisation to bring scattered workers into an industrial system. Nail-making required relatively little capital equipment, a forge and hammer at its simplest, which many rural smiths were easily able to supply. Nail-making required little skill and was straightforward to learn, especially for rural workers who were used to working metal for their agricultural tools.[7] With the opening of the Staffordshire and Worcestershire Canal, from the 1770s, Wombourne had the added advantage of being part of the canal network. This made it easier to transport iron bars and coal into the village and export finished nails from it. The importance of nail-making to Wombourne is indicated by a report to a select committee on workers' conditions in 1888, where it was stated that Wombourne had '1,000 nail shops'.[8] However, it must be noted that as the village's population over the period referred to never rose above 2,000 (men, women and children all included) there must have been some exaggeration in the report.

The bedrock industry in Wombourne up to the nineteenth century must have been agriculture. Domestic service was added to this in the nineteenth century. According to the census returns of the nineteenth century agriculture accounted for approximately 23% of employment across the century, peaking at 26.7% in 1841, declining to just under 20% in 1861 and 1851, but increasing to 25.9% in 1881 before once again declining to 20.9% in 1901. Domestic service averaged 16.6% across the century, building from a low of 13.3% in 1841 to a peak of 20.3% in 1881, before declining to 16.9% in 1901. In absolute numbers agriculture employed between 146 and 206 whilst the numbers employed in domestic service varied from 74 to 161 across the century. Between them, these two industries employed 39.3% of workers on average across the century, with a low of 34.3% in 1861 and a high of 46.2% in 1881.

Other industries developed and contracted across the century, nail-making and iron-and steel-making being the most prominent. In 1841, nail-making employed 32.1% and, in 1851, 33.9% of the workers of the parish, making it the largest single industry in terms of employment at the time. Whole families were involved in the industry: husbands, wives and children. The industry was organised around workshops established in the homes of the workers. Nailers Row in Giggetty Lane is one such example of the arrangement, with a small cottage for living quarters and a forge and workshop to the rear. Whilst the canal eased the transport of iron, coal and other materials into Wombourne, and finished products out, the location of nailers around the parish suggests that it was not essential for the development of the industry in the parish. Nailers are to be found in all parts of the parish, from around the Red Lion public house in the north to Swindon in the south. This perhaps suggests that the industry developed primarily as an addition to the agricultural occupations of the workers rather than as a separate occupation.

Different types of nails were evidently made by different people: for example, some of the workers describe themselves as horse nail-makers. A small number of people give their occupation as nail factor, and there are a number of hardware merchants and their clerks in the censuses, which indicates that these middlemen dealt with the wholesale putting-out process. However, the industry began to decline swiftly in the second half of the nineteenth century, and after 1861 nail factors are no longer to be found in the census. In 1861 there were 231 nailers, 23.7% of the parish workforce; in 1871 this had more than halved and by 1891 the numbers were minuscule. Younger people were moving to other industries: the average age of nail-makers in 1881 was 42, whilst in 1891 the youngest person in the industry was 48.

In 1841 iron- and steel-making employed just over 1% of the parish workforce, and continued at this level until 1861 when the existing

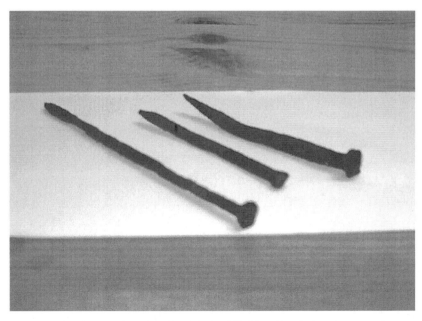

Handmade nails found in the debris of Wellings' workshop (see p. 15).

forge at Swindon was extended. In 1861, 79 people were employed in iron- and steel-making, 8.1% of the parish's total workforce. By 1871 the works was employing 100 people, 12.1% of the workforce, and remained at this level of employment until 1901. Iron- and steel-making never accounted for the same level of employment as did nail-making. In 1841 the two industries together employed 33.4% of the parish workforce, but had declined by 1901 to 13.9%. In 1861 48 (61%) of the 79 workers were living in Swindon, the rest coming from all locations within the parish; of these 30 were newcomers to the village. Of the 31 workers who were not living in Swindon, 13 were new to the village. This suggests that those who moved to the village more often settled close to where they worked. Those who changed occupation were unlikely to also change location if they were already based in the parish.

The core industries of agriculture and manufacturing supported a range of other industries such as saddlery, scythe manufacturing and grinding, wheelwrighting and blacksmithing and transport and construction. Together they created a balanced and locally based economy integrated into the wider national economy through the consumption of raw materials and the outlet of products. Employment in these industries remained roughly static through the nineteenth century. The reduction in employment in iron-, steel- and nail-making was offset by a rise in employment in a range of other industries, reflecting general changes in the British economy. Employment in retail and wholesale endeavours grew from 2.9% in 1841 to 7.2% in 1901 and the percentage employed in the clothes-, shoe- and boot-making trades grew from 2.9% to 6.1%. These changes reflected the growing wealth of the general population in the parish, and also changes to the socio-demographic profile of the village.

Another substantial increase in employment came from the category of general labouring, which in 1901 suddenly accounted for 9.9% of workforce employment; in previous censuses about 4.5% had been employed under this category. This may reflect a change in definitions used in the census, but it may also reflect a general increase in flexibility within the workforce. An individual was less likely to work in one industry, for example agriculture, but, rather, in a broader range of industries, undertaking labouring tasks as required. In the latter part of the nineteenth century, Britain suffered an extended period of slow growth, and the Great Depression starting in the 1870s affected large parts of the economy, especially agriculture and manufacturing.

New industries and employments appeared over the course of the century. Specific to Wombourne was mineral extraction, primarily coal and sand, which increased from zero in 1841 to employ 2.3% of the workforce by 1901. Employment in industries such as education, waterworks, post office, government and services increased altogether

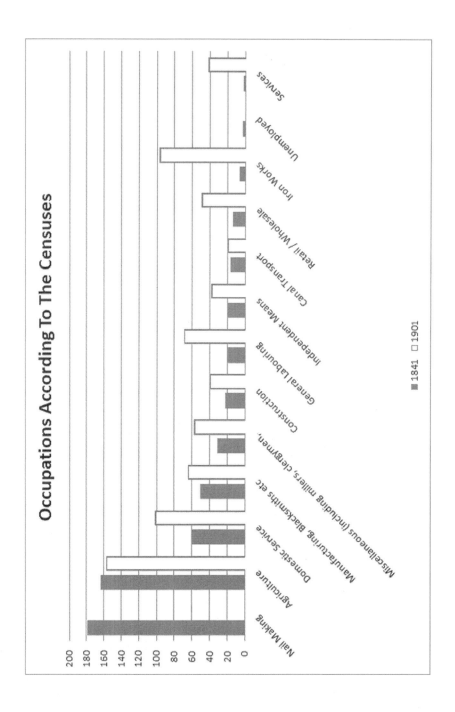

Occupations According To The Censuses

■ 1841   □ 1901

Two views of the railway at Wombourne, dates unknown.

from 0.8% in 1841 to 6.4% in 1901. It is also first noticeable at the end of the nineteenth century that Wombourne was developing as a dormitory town. Inhabitants were working in Wolverhampton and Dudley; John Atherton of Ounsdale Road carried on a business as plumber and gas-fitter in Temple Street, Wolverhampton in 1890[9] and Edwin Steer, who resided in Wombourne, traded as a bacon factor in Great Berry Street, Wolverhampton.[10] However, commuting was not just one way: there is evidence that people lived outside the parish and worked in Wombourne. Matthew Reynolds was working at the tinplate works in Swindon but lived in Wordsley.[11] Other businesses also flourished, but did not grow beyond a small enterprise. For example, William Howell, who in the 1861 census described himself as a 'tailor employing 2 men', advertised every three or four years for a tailor, who could have 'steady employment in Wombourne' from 1866 to 1891.[12] In the 1901 census he is still described as a 'Tailor and Draper', but at the age of 74 he is living alone with his wife, with no mention of servants or staff.

Overall, there was a move away in the nineteenth century from agriculture and manufacturing to a wider range of industries in which the Wombourne workforce was employed. The pace of change seemed to increase in the twentieth century, particularly after the First World War. The construction of a railway linking Wolverhampton to Kidderminster, begun in 1913 and opened to traffic in 1925, brought a small amount of employment to Wombourne and stimulated some local commuting, but the line was essentially a bypass to the heavily used freight routes through Birmingham and the Black Country. The line was never an economic success. It was closed to passenger traffic in 1932 and to freight traffic in 1965; it was dismantled in 1968.[13] Sand-mining at various locations around the parish developed in the later nineteenth century. Sand was used in ironworks to make moulds for the casting of iron parts, often mixed with horse manure and other materials to create the right consistency.[14] The 1881 census records sandpit labourers and a sand merchant for the first time. By 1901 12 people were employed in this industry, including a sand mine manager and three sand merchants. It must be assumed that workers classifying themselves as labourers worked in the sandpits and mines – as well as elsewhere. Sand-mining or quarrying continued into the twentieth century, with sand merchants recorded at Giggetty Wharf.[15] Eventually extensive sandpits were located all across the parish, including very close to the built-up areas of Wombourne and Swindon. However, it is clear that this industry was in decline by the 1940s, as the winding-up of the Bratch Sand Company in 1945 evidenced.[16] Many of the sandpits were left to fill with water and, in an indirect way, became part of the leisure industry of Wombourne when children played in them in the summer months.

Aerial view of Ferro works (note the landmark chimney) adjacent to the canal running under Ounsdale Road.

What eventually became Richard Thomas & Baldwins Ltd, the iron- and steelworks in Swindon, developed along the Staffordshire and Worcestershire Canal. There may have been a forge on the site since the seventeenth century, but the canal provided it with access to pig iron and markets. In 1873 Alfred Baldwin acquired the tinplate works and developed it within the Baldwins' family concern. In 1885 the firm closed their Wolverhampton works and concentrated tinplating at Swindon and Wilden for more 'economical working in tin-plate production'.[17] Into the twentieth century the small-scale flexibility of the works gave it an advantage. As niche markets developed, for example tinplated steel for electric motors, the firm was quickly able to take advantage of the higher margin business. However, as the markets increased, larger businesses, with the economies of scale afforded by their larger production capacities, were able to take them over and margins consequently reduced. Eventually the firm was not able to compete, even as part of the nationalised steel industry and it ceased production in January 1976. Today there is only the canteen left, which has been incorporated into the Community Centre.[18]

The Ferro (Great Britain) Ltd Company was established in 1929 in Ounsdale Road in the house of its first managing director. At first it was a sales outlet for product manufactured in the Netherlands; by 1935 the factory had opened and by the 1970s it was estimated to be the second largest employer in Wombourne after J Timmins' Guardian Safe Company.[19] However, by the end of the twentieth century, the factory had been closed down and the site sold for redevelopment into a housing estate, known locally as 'Fort Apache'. The Guardian Safe Company, which had moved to Wombourne in 1926, relocated to new premises by the ford on Giggetty Lane in 1938. Safes made in Wombourne were exported to all parts of the world, particularly the British Empire. However, by the end of the twentieth century it also was gone. Other businesses entered and left Wombourne: Stronhard-Tremco Ltd leased the old railway buildings in 1968, whilst Midland Aluminium Limited moved and consolidated its production and administration from Wolverhampton into Wombourne in 1960 and 1961.[20]

Planners in the mid-twentieth century wanted to encourage people and businesses to move out of the conurbations and into more pleasant rural districts. Wombourne was a prime site for this due to its rural location, its proximity to Wolverhampton and Dudley and its history of industrial development. Five industrial sites were established, or further developed. On the Bridgnorth Road are the Heath Mill Industrial Estate, the Wombourne Enterprise Park and the Smestow Bridge Industrial Estate; there is another near the junction of Ounsdale Road and Giggetty Lane, and finally there is the small estate on the junction of Planks Lane and Giggetty Lane. There are a wide range of different types of firms on these estates, including builders, double-glazing companies, car repairers, light engineers and potato chip manufacturers. In total there are over 70 businesses on these sites. However, even on these sites change takes place. The site on the junction of Ounsdale Road and Giggetty Lane is earmarked for housing development and many of the businesses have moved, the largest being Solios, part of Fives (an international industrial engineering group). This site specialises in process equipment for the aluminium industry, which has moved to Heath Mill Industrial Estate. On the Heath Mill Industrial Estate, some space has been developed into a large supermarket – and there has been a general turnover of the smaller businesses over time. Service industries have also grown in Wombourne – retail, professional services, and one-man bands providing specialised or local services to the growing population of the parish.

It is difficult to predict how industry will change in the parish as the twenty-first century develops, but change it will.

Notes

1. H. J. Mackinder, 'The Geographical Pivot of History', *The Geographical Journal*, vol. XXIII, no. 4, April (1904), pp. 434–7
2. *Domesday Book: Staffordshire*, tr. and ed. John Morris, (Chichester, Phillimore, 1976), Sections 12,8,3; 12,8,7; 12,8,8
3. Pauline M. Frost, 'The Growth and Localisation of Rural Industry in south Staffordshire 1560–1720' (unpublished doctoral thesis, Polytechnic of Wolverhampton, 1973), p. 573
4. Pauline M. Frost, *op. cit.*, p. 578
5. T. R. Nash, *History of Worcestershire*, p. 57
6. Pauline M. Frost, *op. cit.*, p. 578
7. Pauline M. Frost, *op. cit.*, p. 468
8. *The Victoria History Of The County Of Stafford*, ed. R. B. Pugh (London, Oxford University Press, 1967), p. 241
9. 'Bankruptcy Proceedings', *Birmingham Daily Post,* 15 July 1890, p. 6
10. 'Wolverhampton Bacon Factor Extraordinary Proceedings', *Western Mail*, 31 December 1879, p. 8
11. 'News Of The Week', *The Bristol Mercury and Daily Post,* 22 April 1882
12. 'Situations Vacant', *Birmingham Daily Post*, 18 August 1891
13. *The Victoria History Of The County Of Stafford*, ed. R. B. Pugh (London, Oxford University Press, 1967), p. 241
14. 'Soho Foundry In Retrospect', *The Black Country Bugle*, 9 February 2012
15. *Kelly's Directory of Staffordshire*, 1912
16. *The London Gazette*, 19 October 1945, p. 5144
17. 'The Corn Trade', *Birmingham Daily Post,* 14 September 1885
18. Information kindly provided by Mr C. Robinson of Wombourne
19. *Wombourne Compass*, January 1972
20. 'Midland Aluminium Limited', *The Times*, 13 December 1961